# MELISSA HAYDEN
# OFF STAGE AND ON

PHOTO BY MAURICE SEYMOUR

# Melissa Hayden

## OFF STAGE AND ON

BY MELISSA HAYDEN
PHOTOGRAPHS BY FRED FEHL

DOUBLEDAY & COMPANY, INC.
GARDEN CITY, NEW YORK

Library of Congress Catalog Card Number 63-17277
Copyright © 1963 by Melissa Hayden
All Rights Reserved
Printed in the United States of America

# Foreword

Besides being one of the truly great ballerinas of our era, Melissa Hayden is also one of the most original. She is never satisfied merely to repeat what somebody else has done with a role, but must dig into its roots, discover its real nature, and bring it to flower in terms of her own experience.

Accordingly when she sets out, as she has done in this book, to tell the stories of some of the ballets she has danced, nothing could be further from her habit of thought than just to retell the oft-told plots once more. Instead she must tell what they mean to her as she has studied them and performed them. The way she has chosen to do this is to fit them into a kind of personal diary and thereby allow us to see how they have come to take shape and acquire particular values for her.

Why is it that the same audiences go year after year to such familiar ballets as *Swan Lake* and *Giselle?* The plots and the music are always the same, and the steps never change. Indeed, many of the steps are the same as those done in the ballet classroom day after day. It is only the creative quality brought to them by individual dancers that gives them new life and fresh interest for us each time. Otherwise they would become duller and duller.

But no two really creative ballerinas dance them alike, for the simple reason that no two of them have the same bodies, the same temperaments, or the same personal lives. These are the sources they must draw upon in order to give the stories immediacy and make the choreography something more than just school steps.

Until now no ballerina has thought to tell us how ballets come alive in this way, how they become in a measure almost autobiographical. Miss Hayden's story of her own life in relation to theirs does just that.

JOHN MARTIN

MELISSA HAYDEN
OFF STAGE AND ON

*Portrait Study of Melissa Hayden*

# Nutcracker

Each year at Christmastime the School of American Ballet is filled with anticipation and excitement. The young students do their exercises with extra care. They look up expectantly every time the classroom door opens, for the ballet mistress of the New York City Ballet is coming. Within a few days a list of names will be posted on the school bulletin board and the children whose names appear on that list are invited to dance with the New York City Ballet in its annual Christmas production, *The Nutcracker*.

As the city puts on its holiday dress of Christmas decorations the *Nutcracker* children put on practice clothes and ballet slippers and work for many long hours in the rehearsal rooms and theater. They will soon be entering a new world of stage doors and dressing rooms, of make-up and audiences.

As a ballerina of the New York City Ballet, I dance the lead in almost all the sixty different ballets the company performs except *The Nutcracker*. The star of *The Nutcracker* is a young student whose name in the ballet is Clara. I dance the role of the Sugar Plum Fairy.

From the time Clara is chosen until her first performance she hasn't a moment to herself. She is busy with rehearsals, costume fittings, ballet classes, and publicity releases. During any spare time she must keep up with her regular schoolwork. When she has finally mastered the steps of the ballet, there are rehearsals with the full company on the stage, rehearsals with the orchestra, and rehearsals with the stage hands. She must learn where all the different props and scenery are on stage and how to navigate through the difficult set. There is so much for her to do that there is no time for her to be nervous.

The day of the performance is different. There is nothing to do except wait. The stage hands must have the stage for their final technical rehearsal. Clara comes to the theater early, hoping that she can find some quiet corner backstage to rehearse by herself. But there is no quiet corner during *Nutcracker* season.

Backstage is filled with forty children, forty sets of parents, and younger brothers and sisters who couldn't be left home alone. There are sixty members of the regular company, wardrobe women, stage hands, people delivering flowers and telegrams. Clara walks into this crowded excitement and becomes frightened. She goes to the large dressing room, which she shares with the other children, puts on her make-up, and tries to sit quietly and think about her steps. I know from experience that the minute you begin to think about a performance every step disappears from your mind, and mentally you trip and fall so many times that you become sore from imaginary black-and-blue marks.

I come early too because I find it important to spend a few hours in the atmosphere of the theater before a performance. For me, there is such a difference between the outside world and the world on stage that I need time for the effects of one to wear off to be able to enter the other. I know how Clara must be feeling and, since my dressing room is alone and quiet, I ask her if she would like to share it with me.

Clara tries to hide her nervousness. For some reason she doesn't think it is professional or grown up, but she looks very pale despite her full stage make-up. "Is my make-up all right,

Miss Hayden?" she asks. It usually is, but I remind her that she will have to change it slightly for the second act. In the second act, the lights change from blues to ambers and, unless you wear more rouge than usual, the amber lights make you look pale. "Miss Hayden," she asks timidly, "were you very nervous when you danced Clara long ago?"

I tell her that when I was twelve years old there was no New York City Ballet, no production of *The Nutcracker* in which students could get performance experience. I didn't know then that I wanted to be a dancer. I had not taken a single ballet lesson.

I was very shy and didn't speak very often. I wanted to be a writer. I used to write for hours in my diary and dream that someday I would speak to people through my books. I never dreamed, when my best girl friend asked me to take ballet lessons with her, that I would discover a way of speaking through dance and movement.

At first I thought ballet would consist of pretty steps and I was disappointed because my teacher would not let me move freely and dance. He kept me at the barre almost all the time during the first year, doing the same exercises sixteen or twenty times every day in the same exact disciplined manner.

After a while I began to get a strange feeling. I felt silly and too shy to mention it but these precise, unvaried exercises seemed to be giving me a sense of freedom. I started to look forward to my lessons, and when my Thursday class was over it seemed as though the next Tuesday's lesson would never come.

My new feeling of freedom wasn't confined to the ballet class alone. Instead of being a shy quiet girl at home, I would come whooping in from school and go running through our house, sticking my nose into pots on the stove, singing loudly, and in general shouting exuberantly at the top of my voice to my mother or father or my two sisters. My mother told me later that I had the most raucous voice she had ever heard and she used to shudder when I came home from school. She never said anything then because she was so pleased that I was losing my shyness.

I noticed something else, and last Christmas when I told Clara about it in the dressing room, she said she had noticed the same thing about herself. Before I started taking ballet lessons I was very busy and never seemed to have any time. I was taking two programs in high school, both academic and commercial. My mother and father thought I should prepare myself for a job, so I took the commercial course, which consisted of bookkeeping, typing and shorthand, and business English. But I wanted to go to college when I graduated from high school, so I arranged to take a full academic program as well. I was also on the swimming team and practiced four times a week. It was a very hard schedule, but when I added two ballet lessons a week and worked even harder it seemed as if I had more time instead of less. I was so happy!

Clara told me that she was taking music lessons, was on the cheerleaders' squad, and was a student representative, but despite all this and her busy schedule with *Nutcracker,* she found more time now to read or just sit and talk to her mother and father.

We both agreed that, when you are doing something you love more than anything else, the rest of your life seems much simpler and yet fuller.

As we spoke, Clara was relaxing. Her face looked even younger beneath her make-up. I knew that worse than nervousness is a feeling of complete relaxation before a performance. I have seen more than one "relaxed" performer break into tears when the first notes of the orchestra suddenly told them the performance was really beginning.

I had to bring Clara back to the performance, but gently through the right kind of concentration on her role.

"You know what I do before each performance?" I asked her.

"No," she said.

"I study my roles by telling myself in words the story of the ballet I will soon be telling in movement on the stage. I make up word stories about the ballets, and these stories give me a deeper understanding of the character I am going to portray. It helps me to recall the steps in a way I never could if I tried to think about them separately. Why don't you tell me the story of *Nutcracker* in words as you will tell the story in dance on the stage?"

"But I wouldn't know how to do that," Clara said, and she was frightened again.

"I'll show you how I do it. I'll tell you the story of *Nutcracker* the way I would tell it on stage if I were dancing the role of Clara."

Before I tell the story of a ballet to myself, I think about the girl I am supposed to be on stage. I find out what part of me is like her, what experiences I have had in my life that will help me understand her. That way I am never completely acting on stage, for the character is a small part of my own life. Thinking about the part of Clara in *Nutcracker* will be fun because I have to go back and remember myself as I was when I was a ballet student.

I was fourteen years old when I decided to become a dancer. I had been studying ballet for almost two years but I had never seen a ballet company perform. In those days very few touring companies came to Toronto, Canada, where I lived. We were all very excited at the ballet school when our teacher told us that the Ballet Theatre Company was coming to Toronto. I went rushing home, even noisier than usual, and asked my mother if I could go. She said yes and the next day I went downtown and bought myself a ticket.

A light snow was falling on the night of the performance. As I rode downtown, I kept rubbing a little bare place on the frosted streetcar window so that I could look out. I was happy that Toronto was dressed in sparkling white to welcome the Ballet Theatre. I arrived at the theater early and bought a souvenir program book to read. There were pictures of all the dancers in their different costumes. Many of them had long Russian names and I was dismayed at my short Canadian name.

Soon the curtain went up. I watched the performance with the critical eye that only a beginning ballet student can have. How correctly she points her toe, I thought. . . . Oh no, that isn't right, her foot didn't pass through first position. But as I watched, the detail began to blur. I no longer saw steps or even individual dancers. All I knew was that somehow the magic combination of music and dance was speaking to me from the stage and my answer was an intensity of feeling and emotion such as I had never experienced.

After the performance I walked home. Movement had become so much a part of life for me that I felt I had to keep moving to understand what had happened on stage and inside of me. Now I understood the meaning of what I had felt in my ballet class. No wonder that every time I did an exercise I felt a sense of freedom. I wasn't learning steps, I was learning words. I was learning a new vocabulary. I knew that I would practice and practice so that I could make sentences of the words I was learning. Someday I would say these sentences with my body on a stage and speak to an audience. I decided that I must become a dancer. I began to walk faster. The cold night air made my nose tingle and feel warm.

There was no doubt in my mind that I would succeed but I

began to feel impatient. I was fourteen years old. I had only been studying ballet for two years—not six or seven years like the other students. I was at least four years behind and I had to catch up.

I started taking four lessons a week. I used to travel two hours a day, back and forth on the streetcar to downtown Toronto where the ballet school was located. I didn't mind the ride. I did my homework on the streetcar. I took my classes with a fierce determination to catch up. Every time I did an exercise I thought of it as putting a penny in the bank account which would grow slowly each and every day until I was rich in ballet training.

My technique began to grow but I was learning bad habits. The determination and impatience were beginning to show in my dancing. I wanted so much to learn that I was fighting the steps instead of dancing them. Later, when I became a performer, I had the same fault. It took me many years to get over being a personality on stage and to mature into being an artist.

Clara and I both laughed as I told her I thought I would have been terrible as Clara in *Nutcracker* when I was a young girl. The role requires a lovable, charming quality which my impatience did not allow me to have then. I wondered if I would have been wise enough to know that, had I been given the opportunity to dance Clara when I was fourteen years old. "If I had been wise enough," I said to Clara, "this is the story of *Nutcracker* as I would have told it then on stage."

## The Story

On Christmas Eve my brother Fritz and I came inside from playing in the snow. Mother said we had to go right upstairs to rest or we would be too tired for the party that evening. I was very excited because this Christmas I had made up my mind to see who really trimmed the Christmas tree and put the presents underneath it. Fritz had always told me it was Mother and Daddy and not Santa Claus, but until that year I had not believed him.

For some reason, this year it seemed that he might be telling the truth. I wanted to see for myself. I wondered if I would mind if there weren't a Santa Claus. I went upstairs and changed into my party dress. Even though I was very sleepy, I tiptoed down again. Thinking back, it seems to me that a wonderful adventure started then and there, but at the time nothing seemed strange at all.

When I got downstairs I saw that Fritz was there ahead of me. His face was pressed to the keyhole of the living-room door. "See," he said, "there is no Santa Claus," and through the keyhole I saw Mother and Daddy on high ladders hanging the ornaments on the Christmas tree.

I ran over to the big couch, sat down, and cried. Fritz said that he had cried too when he found out there was no Santa Claus. I felt better and then I did not mind too much, for after all my own mother and father were more wonderful than any Santa Claus could be. I guess I must have fallen asleep there because the next thing I knew I awoke and it was dark outside. Fritz was asleep next to me, his head in my lap.

I touched Fritz gently and when he woke up I went back to look through the keyhole again. Mother and Daddy were just finishing decorating the tree and the maids were straightening up the living room. Fritz was very grumpy because I woke him and he kept pulling me away from the keyhole so he could look. We were having fun wrestling back and forth when the doorbell rang and the first guests began to arrive.

Our friends sat with us outside in the big hall while their parents had a chance to put their presents underneath the tree. I was with the girls in one group, talking about the Christmas gifts we would receive. We knew we were going to get dolls because we had asked most often for them but we wondered what else there would be. Fritz and the boys sat in another circle, talking about toy guns, bugles, and drums. They were always playing soldier and pretending they were in the army.

Soon our parents called us into the big room. We all marveled when they opened the door. The lights in the room were all turned off, except the lights on the Christmas tree itself. They sparkled and glittered back and forth between the gaily colored ornaments till it seemed that the tree was alive with dancing colors. A little angel on the top of the tree smiled at me as the lights flitted across her face. What a marvelous time I was having.

Next we opened our presents and I got the most beautiful doll you have ever seen. She had real golden hair you could comb, and she was dressed in the prettiest dress with three real lace petticoats underneath. The other girls had dolls too and we showed them to each other and played together. The boys were blowing their bugles and hitting their drums till I thought I had never heard so much noise. Their fathers thought the same thing because they very sternly told them to be quiet.

Just then the room had one of those funny stillnesses when everyone stops talking at the same time. Our big grandfather clock began to strike the hour of eight. Everyone was startled because it was so loud in the midst of so much quiet. We have a very strange grandfather clock. It has a huge owl on top and, whenever the clock strikes, the owl flaps its wings. The clock hoots like an owl instead of going Boom Boom Boom like all my friends' clocks. When I was younger, I sometimes thought the owl was going to swoop down from the clock and grab me up in his claws.

As the clock stopped striking and the owl went back to sleep for another hour, the doorbell rang and Herr Drosselmeyer came in. He was the man who had made our funny owl clock and I thought he was most peculiar. Daddy said he was an inventor as well as a clockmaker, and each Christmas he made the most wonderful toys. But he also always brought us something very scary. The previous Christmas he had brought a wonderful merry-go-round with horses that pranced around and little toy boys and girls who rode them. We laughed and giggled as they pranced around. But then he brought out a fierce mechanical cat that chased little toy mice and gobbled them up. I did not think that was funny at all, even though he showed me that the mice were not hurt and we could play the game again. I was glad when Fritz accidentally broke the toy.

When Herr Drosselmeyer came this year, he brought with him three of the largest boxes I had ever seen, and we could not wait to see what presents were inside. In fact, I was so interested in the boxes that I did not notice the young man who had come with him. It was not until he introduced his nephew Franz that I really saw him. He was very handsome and very polite and I liked him. He was the same age as Fritz but very different. Fritz was seldom quiet but Franz stood quietly watching all that was happening around him.

Franz helped Herr Drosselmeyer move the boxes to the center of the room and then Herr Drosselmeyer opened the first two boxes. There were two dolls inside that actually danced ballet. They were just like the dancers I had seen at the opera house. All the girls loved them. Then he opened the other box and out came a toy soldier who marched up and down and saluted. The boys like him. Herr Drosselmeyer was very funny. He flapped his coattails at the toys when their dance was over and shooed them back into their boxes. He seemed like a big bird flapping his wings . . . like the owl on top of the clock.

Then Herr Drosselmeyer entertained us with some magic tricks. Just as I was thinking there would be nothing scary this year, he pulled from somewhere underneath the big folds of his coat the funniest nutcracker with the ugliest face I ever saw. "This is for you, Clara," he said, and when I looked up

*He pulled from somewhere underneath the big folds of his coat the funniest nutcracker with the ugliest face I ever saw*

into his face to thank him, I saw him looking at me in the strangest way. "I have been watching you for many Christmases and now I think you are ready to receive this handsome prince."

Everyone laughed because, of course, the Nutcracker was not handsome, but somehow I could not laugh. I thought the Nutcracker must be very sad to have such an ugly face, and then I thought of the story of the prince who was changed into an ugly frog. If I loved him very much, I thought, maybe the Nutcracker would really become a handsome prince just as Herr Drosselmeyer said. I felt very warm and good inside and when I looked up from my Nutcracker again, I noticed Franz, Herr Drosselmeyer's nephew, watching me with his serious eyes. I could tell he understood how I felt and I was very grateful to him.

My brother Fritz was angry. He wanted the Nutcracker and, when Herr Drosselmeyer gave it to me instead of to him, he began to frown and sulk. Without warning, he grabbed the Nutcracker from my hands and threw him on the floor and stepped on him.

"Oh, my poor Nutcracker," I said as I bent over him. "His arm is broken." I picked him up and held him close to me so he would not feel the pain too much and I cried. Herr Drosselmeyer came over and made a sling for my wounded Nutcracker. He promised me quietly that if I put the Nutcracker to sleep beneath the Christmas tree the good fairies would come during the night and make him well again. His nephew brought me my doll's bed and together we put my wounded prince to sleep.

Our guests began to leave, but Herr Drosselmeyer and his nephew stayed till last. I was glad because it gave me a chance to be with them longer. Franz and I held each other's hands for a long time when we said good-by, and it was all I could do

*If I loved him very much I thought maybe the nutcracker would be-*
*come a handsome prince*

to keep from calling to him as I saw him walk toward the door.

"Don't worry, little princess," he said, "we will see each other again soon." I liked him to call me little princess and I hoped with all my heart that we would indeed see each other soon again.

I went upstairs and got ready for bed. As I said my prayers I heard the big owl clock strike eleven and I became frightened. Suppose the good fairies could not find out what was wrong with my Nutcracker? He would need me with him to tell them.

Once again I tiptoed downstairs. I took my Nutcracker out of the doll's bed. I held him in my arms and together we lay down on the big couch to wait for the good fairies to come.

A little later I heard a noise; it was my mother coming into the room to look for me. She must have gone into the bedroom to kiss me good night and seen that I was not in bed.

I closed my eyes and made believe I was asleep so that she would not make me leave. I felt her cover me with the shawl from her shoulders and quietly say, "Good night, Clara." It was all I could do not to kiss her for being so sweet and letting me stay but I still made believe I was asleep.

When she left I became very drowsy but I kept saying over and over again, "I must not fall asleep. I must not fall asleep."

My words seemed to make me even sleepier. There was a noise from the living-room door. I saw the door open, and Herr Drosselmeyer entered. I heard his slow heavy steps as he walked across the room and paused at the Christmas tree.

He muttered to himself and then I heard him say more loudly, "There she is holding her Nutcracker. I wonder if she is worthy of the journey I have planned for her. Only if she is brave enough." Then he repeated, "Only if she is brave enough . . ." and "I wonder."

I was not sure what he meant but I knew at that moment that I was not brave. The only reason I did not run away was because I was too frightened to move.

I heard Herr Drosselmeyer's footsteps coming toward me once more. He sat down on the couch next to me. He seemed satisfied that I was asleep and took the Nutcracker from my arms. I opened my eyes just a little and watched him start to mend the Nutcracker's arm. He seemed to love the Nutcracker as much as I, and I was no longer frightened. Then Herr Drosselmeyer began talking to the Nutcracker. "There, my prince, you are well again. Good! You must be in perfect condition. You have a difficult journey ahead of you. You must defend our princess and take her to the Kingdom of the Sweets." I kept trying to hear what he was saying but I was so sleepy.

When Herr Drosselmeyer finished mending the Nutcracker he placed him back in my arms and covered us again with the warm shawl Mother had put over me. I kept my eyes shut and listened to him as he walked across the room. How strange, I thought. His footsteps have stopped but I did not hear the big door open or feel that funny chilly draft as before when he opened the door.

Suddenly the door opened by itself. A huge mouse, bigger even than Fritz, walked into the room on his hind legs. I held my breath. He looked around all over the room. It seemed forever. And then he left. Thank goodness he didn't see me.

Then the owl clock struck twelve, and when I looked, I could not take my eyes off it. On the top of the clock where the owl used to be was Herr Drosselmeyer. He was all hunched up like the owl and flapping his coattails like the owl's wings. He seemed to be calling to the toys. He motioned to the Christmas tree and the lights started blinking and blinking. He waved his arms and the tree started growing and growing. Bigger and bigger, up and up went the tree. And when it touched the walls and ceiling they dissolved into air and I was left standing in my nightdress in the middle of a big field!

Then I saw all about me, lined up for battle, a battalion of toy soldiers. "Don't worry," they said, "we will protect you."

I was glad they were there. They looked brave and strong. A little toy rabbit was their drummer boy. He was the only one who seemed afraid. "Where is the General?" he asked. "Where is the General?"

Then my doll's bed came wheeling in like a chariot—only

it was as large as a real bed, and on it was my friend the Nutcracker! He was grown up and he was dressed as the general
of the army. His ugly face seemed beautiful, but very stern and
ferocious, and I had to laugh a little at my dear little Nutcracker being so fierce. I wondered what would happen next
but I did not have long to wait.

The big mouse returned but this time brought with him a
whole army of huge mice. Their king was leading them and he
was terrible to look at. He had seven heads, each one more evil
than the other, and on each was a jeweled crown. All the mice
scared me, but he scared me most of all.

The mice started marching and the soldiers began to fire.
Wherever the soldiers fired the mice fell dead, but each time
the soldiers turned their backs the mice got up and started
toward them again.

The Nutcracker, sword in hand, kept running in front of
our troops, cheering them on and keeping up their courage.
Despite their courage, the soldiers could not kill the mice, and
the mice began to carry off the soldiers, one by one. I looked
around and saw the king of the mice coming straight for me.
In a moment he would have me. Then the little toy rabbit
showed he was truly brave. He rushed up and as the mouse
king was bending over me pulled his tail.

The mouse turned away from me. He seemed very confused
that anyone would dare pull his kingly tail. Looking around, he
spied the Nutcracker lying unconscious on the ground. He began to walk toward him very purposefully and lifted his
sword, prepared to kill him as he lay there. I knew I had to do
something to get his attention. There was little time. I took
off my shoe and threw it and hit the king of the mice in the
middle of the back. He stopped advancing on the Nutcracker
and turned around in a rage.

Then he spied me and began running toward me, brandish-

*The nutcracker was dressed as the general of the army*

ing his sword. He raised his sword over me, and his face was so close to mine that I could count every single one of his whiskers. I thought that all was finished with me. But then I saw the Nutcracker get up and come rushing toward us. He reached us just in time and ran the mouse king through with his sword. The king fell dead and the battle was over.

Then all the mice began to cry and I began to feel sorry for them. "Why did you kill our king?" they kept sobbing. "Why did you kill our king? We weren't going to hurt you. We were only trying to frighten you."

The Nutcracker took the topmost crown from the highest head of the mouse king and placed it on my head. "Now you are really Princess Clara," he said. He sounded just like Franz when he said good-by to me earlier in the evening. "You have saved my life," he said, "and by your bravery you have passed the last of the tests that have been set for you. You are a very brave girl."

I really felt like a princess. I thanked the Nutcracker for the crown. As my first command as Princess Clara, I said, "I command you to become a handsome prince."

The Nutcracker answered me, "Yes, Princess Clara, I shall become a handsome prince, and it shall all be your doing because you love me so much and because you are so brave. And I shall take you on a wonderful journey to a land where only the kindest and bravest and most loving boys and girls can go."

"But why can't you become a prince now?" I asked him.

"Have faith, Princess Clara," he replied. "Lie on your bed and rest, and just remember to be very brave and to continue to love me very much."

Then he walked off, growing smaller and smaller, as he became a part of the distance. Though I called to him many times, he would not turn around.

I lay down on my huge doll's bed and began to cry. I love him, I love him, I kept thinking to myself. I kept my eyes tightly shut, and it seemed as if the bed was moving. And then I began to feel cold, and I felt little snowflakes falling on my face and nose. But I remembered what the Nutcracker said and I would not open my eyes. I don't care if I freeze or if this bed moves all the way to the North Pole, I will keep my eyes closed and continue to love my Nutcracker. When he comes back, he will be a prince.

Faintly, I heard a voice calling "Princess Clara, Princess Clara." I opened my eyes and saw my Nutcracker. I looked at him and before my eyes he turned into a handsome prince.

He looked just like Herr Drosselmeyer's nephew Franz, and I wasn't surprised at all.

I said to him, "Thank you for coming for me, Prince Franz."

"Thank you for loving me so much, Princess Clara," he replied.

"How did you become the Nutcracker?" I asked.

Then he explained to me that his uncle had magical powers to make good little boys and girls very happy. He told me that every Christmas he chose one child and sent him or her to visit a far-off magic land called the Kingdom of the Sweets.

But first he always tested the child. And he had tested me to see if I was really good and brave and loyal to my toys and dolls. He said that Herr Drosselmeyer knew I was very good to my dolls, for he had watched me every Christmas. He also knew I was brave, for I had saved the Nutcracker's life during the battle with the mice. And when he saw how I loved my Nutcracker, he was convinced I loved my toys. He sent Franz for me and arranged that I should visit the wonderful Kingdom of the Sweets.

"But what is the Kingdom of the Sweets?" I asked Franz.

"It is a magic land," Franz said, "all covered with snow, but it is never cold. When we get there you will be met by a lovely lady called the Sugar Plum Fairy, who rules the land."

I asked him to tell me as much as he knew.

"Angels will serve you a banquet of ice cream and candy, and you can eat as much as you want. You will never get sick or have an upset stomach in the Kingdom of the Sweets!

"Toys from all over the world live in the Kingdom before they go to earth to make children happy, and all these toys will perform for you. Even the dewdrops will dance for you before they leave for earth to make the morning grass glisten with their kisses. And, most beautiful of all, when the day is over and just before you leave for home, the Sugar Plum Fairy

*Beauty will walk with you for the rest of your life*

herself will dance for you. Her prince will dance with her and it will be the most beautiful sight you will ever see.

"When you are older and a young lady, if you shut your eyes and imagine the Sugar Plum Fairy dancing, you will see her, and because you do, you will always be lovely. Beauty will walk with you for the rest of your life."

"Oh, Franz," I said, "let's go."

He took my hand and we walked off together through snowflakes that danced like fairies about us. Soon we came to the boat that would sail through the heavens and take us to the Kingdom of the Sweets.

*Snowflakes danced like fairies about us*

# Afternoon of a Faun

When I have finished telling Clara the story of *Nutcracker* it is time for her to go down to the stage for her performance. I do not make my entrance until the second act, and I have an hour to spend alone in my dressing room. There are always many chores for me to do. There are toe shoes to darn, tights to mend, and practice clothes to wash. I like to sew in my dressing room before a performance. Being occupied with my hands makes me feel less nervous, yet sewing is so automatic that my mind is free to wander and think about my different roles.

I pick up a pair of practice tights. There is a hole in the knee that I must mend. As I begin to sew I think about *Afternoon of a Faun*. I want to give some more thought to my interpretation of the ballet.

There are two different ballets called *Afternoon of a Faun*. The older version is about a faun and a group of nymphs who meet and play in a pasture in ancient Greece. This was the version Nijinsky made famous. The *Afternoon of a Faun* that I dance with the New York City Ballet is about a boy and a girl who, one hot summer day, find themselves alone in a ballet studio.

A mirror covers the front wall. Dancers must look at themselves while they practice to see how their movements will look to an audience. In ballet the dancer creates pictures. The space around her is her background and frame.

The girl in the ballet never takes her eyes off the mirror. She insists on perfection. Any time she sees a "line" in the mirror that is harsh or not in perfect harmony with the rest of her body, she stretches an arm just a little more so that she will look longer and more graceful, or turns out a leg so that all the planes of her body are in perfect harmony. Through this continuous self-appraisal she hopes to make each picture she presents to an audience the ultimate in beauty.

The girl in the ballet and I are very much alike. I work for perfection too. Not only do I study myself in the mirror while I am practicing but I study other pictures in space which help me understand the beauty of "line." I look at tall buildings, modern bridges, and new cars. I see how great designers and architects have placed these structures as pictures in a frame of the world about them. When I go back to my rehearsal room and mirror I am better able to understand what is required of me in ballet.

Sometimes I study my image in the mirror so objectively that I think the girl in the mirror is someone else. I get impatient with her when she does not do a step correctly and praise her when she dances well.

The girl in the ballet never gets over this strange feeling of being two people. In real life I do, for to me it is only a means of becoming a better dancer.

Quietly I allow the romantic Debussy music of the ballet to play through my mind.

I think I understand why I have not been completely satisfied with my interpretation of the girl in *Faun*. I have been allowing the romantic quality of the music to decide the overall mood of the ballet. But *Faun* is not a romantic story of a boy and a girl. I have not been taking into account the strange unrealness of a girl who never sees life other than as a reflection in a mirror.

*Not only do I study myself in the mirror while I am practicing but I study other pictures in space which help me understand the beauty of "line"*

I know what I must do. I must change my vision of the re-hearsal room where I am supposed to meet the boy. I have always thought of it as a room at the School of American Ballet, because I do so much rehearsing there. But it can't be. The rooms are too bright and cheerful, with light streaming through the skylight and the walls freshly painted. It has to be some place more mysterious, a place so isolated that, once I am inside, there might not even be an outside world to tell me the girl in the mirror is really I.

I think about all the places in which I've rehearsed since I began to dance. There have been so many of them. One of them must be the right place for *Afternoon of a Faun.*

It can't be the studio where I took lessons in Toronto. In those days there was never a time when I was not with other children. But that was the only rehearsal room I knew when I was a student. I shall have to find a room further on in my career.

When I graduated from high school I wanted to leave To-ronto and study with more advanced teachers but I had no money and my father did not think I should be alone in a strange city.

Now I was glad I had taken that commercial course in high school. I was able to get a job and in two years I had saved enough for a train ticket to New York City and for three months of study there. After that I would get another job. I hoped it would be dancing and not an office job.

I asked my ballet teacher to speak to my father, hoping he would say I had enough talent to make a career of dancing and would help convince him that I should be allowed to continue my studies away from home. He told me he would not because he didn't think I was ready for more advanced training.

His words made me fearful. I had no way of comparing my

ability with other professional dancers and I thought I might get to New York only to find out that I could not succeed. I felt lonely at the thought of failing far from home.

For just a moment I considered giving up my plans but then I decided I must find out for myself. Even though I did not have my teacher's blessing, I *did* have my own knowledge of six years of hard work and study. That would have to be enough.

My mother was wonderful at that time. She spent many a night talking to my father and trying to convince him that I should have my chance. Finally he consented and I left for New York. One of my happiest moments was his look of pride many years later when he came backstage after a performance with the New York City Ballet.

I worked very hard in New York. I studied with many different teachers and in many different schools. Wherever I went I was placed in the advanced class and my frightened feeling soon disappeared as I saw I was being accepted as an advanced student.

At the end of three months of study in New York my money ran out and I auditioned for a job at Radio City Music Hall. I was accepted as a member of the corps de ballet and I breathed a sigh of relief at the thought of the weekly pay check that would assure my future studies in New York.

But I didn't have much time for study. I danced in four shows a day with only two hours off between shows. I used to dash out of the theater with full make-up on, race to my ballet class, and then rush back just in time to make my entrance on stage.

I didn't get a chance to do much real dancing at the Music Hall because I always seemed to have a half a dozen light bulbs connected to my costume which would light up at various times throughout the ballet. Once I was a light that twinkled on a Christmas tree and another time I was the forty-sixth star in the American flag.

I went to the library and learned that the forty-sixth star was Oklahoma. After that, every time I went on stage I was not only a light, I was saying, "I am Oklahoma; I was admitted to the Union on November 16, 1907; and I am a great producer of oil." Of course I didn't think anyone would know what I was saying but I had made up my mind that the only way I could learn to express myself was always to know what I was supposed to be on stage and what I wanted to say. I was preparing myself for the important roles I hoped to dance.

After six months at Radio City I felt I was ready for my real goal: to dance in a ballet company.

I auditioned for Ballet Theatre and was accepted as a member of the corps de ballet. I was happy. Ever since that snowy night when I had seen them perform in Toronto, I had wanted to dance with them.

Ballet Theatre was a touring company and I was sorry to leave New York and my classes. I knew that while playing one-night stands I would have little opportunity to study but I also knew I had to get more performance experience. I toured with Ballet Theatre for more than two and a half years and left them only because the company disbanded for a time.

On my first six-month tour with Ballet Theatre we performed in more than eighty-six cities all over the United States. We traveled by train or bus, leaving after our performance at night or early next morning, arriving in the new town sometime in the afternoon. When we arrived we rehearsed or took ballet class and then put on our make-up for the evening performance.

Many of the cities in which we performed did not have theaters. Sometimes we danced in high school auditoriums, sometimes in movie theaters or local civic centers. We could not use these stages for rehearsals because the stage hands had barely enough time to do everything necessary for the evening performance, and there weren't any rehearsal rooms. At different times during that tour we rehearsed in high school chemistry laboratories, grand ballrooms of hotels, and in nice weather even outside on the school handball courts.

None of these places fit the mood of *Afternoon of a Faun*. I continue my search for that rehearsal room.

As the first tour with Ballet Theatre was coming to a close I was very excited. The last week of the tour we would be performing in New York City at the Metropolitan Opera House. I was looking forward to that. There was so much tradition at the Met. I loved watching operas there, sitting in the deep red plush seats and glancing around the elegant house to which the signs of age had added dignity.

I begin to think about my first rehearsal at the Met and suddenly I get an eerie feeling. It is the exact feeling I want for *Afternoon of a Faun*. What happened at that first rehearsal?

I remember my excitement. I was being given my first solo role. The corps de ballet was rehearsing on stage. The ballet master told one of the older girls to take me and three of the other soloists to the rehearsal rooms on the fifth floor and teach us our parts.

I followed the girl to an old elevator that moaned and groaned as it jerked us upward. There were no sides to the elevator and the walls of the shaft were thick with grime. At the fifth floor I followed the girl off into a dimly lit narrow corridor that wound in an aimless pattern. Along its sides lurked dark open doorways. Grotesque shapes beckoned from these caverns. I shuddered as I walked by. It didn't help when I realized they were only the storage rooms where old trunks and scenery and costumes from the operas were stored. I thought of the Phantom of the Opera leaping at me from one of those dark opera graveyards, and I hurried so that I was no longer last in line. I was not the only one affected by this atmosphere. I noticed that, even though the other girls had taken this walk before, they too were strangely silent.

We walked up a flight of steps and through a dark room to a big metal door. We stepped through the door and when it clanged hollowly shut behind us, I found myself on a narrow catwalk that swayed with every step I took. Looking down between the flimsy handrail and the catwalk, I could see the rest of the company on stage, five long flights below. I was crossing high over the Metropolitan Opera House stage and I was frightened. Finally we reached the other side and another metal door that led to the rehearsal room we were to use. When I stepped through that door I felt I was entering the protected comfort of another world.

I am looking forward to my next performance of *Afternoon of a Faun*. Now that I have placed the ballet in that quiet rehearsal room, it seems there is so much more I can do to capture the mood of the work.

I decide not to wait till I perform the ballet again. I'll tell myself the story of *Faun* in words, as I have done so many times before, only this time, before I start, I will walk across an imaginary catwalk high above the stage of the Metropolitan Opera House and as I make my entrance on the stage I will hear a heavy metal door creak slowly and then close with a hollow clang behind me.

# The Story

It was hot that day in July. I came early to the studio so that I could be alone and practice some steps from the new ballet I was learning. As I entered the room I was at once faced by the huge mirror that covered one wall. I looked at myself in the mirror as if there was another person there. I tightened my belt. The girl in the mirror tightened hers. I touched my hair. The other girl touched hers too. It was a funny little game I played by myself and I enjoyed it. The girl in the mirror enjoyed it too, but never let it show by any expression on her face.

I began to walk to the center of the floor, watching the girl in the mirror as she followed me. She moved with her knees properly turned out, toes pointed and head carried well on her shoulders. I liked this girl I saw in the mirror.

Suddenly I was startled by another reflection in the mirror. It took me a moment to realize there was a boy in the room. He was lying on the floor and must have been watching me all the time. The little game I had been playing seemed very childish to me now, and I thought it must seem very conceited to him.

I looked at the girl in the mirror. She seemed completely at ease. Her lithe dancer's body was arranged in that seemingly effortless pose all dancers assume when they are standing still on stage. Then I saw her begin to move toward the side of the room. I was surprised but I followed her to the barre and began warming up as she did.

I was glad she thought of doing our exercises because if I had stayed much longer in the center of the room I would have had to say something, and I was a little afraid of him as I was of most boys. I gave all my concentration to the work I was doing. Gradually the comfort of my muscles in the familiar routine of my exercises spread to my mind and I was able to look at the boy in the mirror and wonder about him. I wondered what he must think as he watched me. "What a lovely dancer. She must love dancing very much to come early to the studio to practice." I thought he must love dancing too, and I wanted very much to dance with him. I imagined he would invent beautiful steps and lifts as we danced together and I would follow him perfectly, anticipating his every movement.

As if sensing my thought, the boy in the mirror got up and walked toward the girl in the mirror. Effortlessly, he lifted her in the air and to my amazement my feet were no longer on the ground. I knew, of course, that the girl in the mirror was only a reflection of me but somehow it was safer to think of her as a separate person. Gently he lowered her feet to the ground.

Dancing together, they were one. Each movement he made was strong and masculine with a beginning and an end. The girl moved with the quiet serenity that only hour after hour of practice can achieve. The lines of their bodies complemented each other. Each step they took created a different picture in space—a kaleidoscope of modern paintings whose planes and angles were in perfect composition and harmony.

I never took my eyes off the mirror. I was in love with the couple dancing there. I loved the feeling of commanding my

*Effortlessly he lifted her in the air*

body to move and watching another body obey my command. I sensed the same feeling in the boy next to me, but all that showed on our faces was quiet concentration in our movements and in each other. Slowly my enjoyment in watching the mirror became a need. I could not turn away. I could not

*Each step they took created a different picture in space*

look directly at this boy of whose warm body I was conscious. I felt that if I saw him other than from the safety of reflection, his warmth would be too intense and I would melt from sheer happiness. I felt as if there were no floor and no room, just a cool clear mirror of wonderment and reflection.

Suddenly I saw the girl in the mirror lifted high in the air and disappear. I couldn't understand where she had gone. Then I realized the boy had lifted me and turned me away from the mirror. I was held high over his head and I had no mirror to look into. I looked down and there were his eyes, clear eyes . . . friendly eyes. Playfully my feet danced in the air. They were saying, "Thank you for turning me away from the mirror. Thank you for making me look into the eyes of a real boy." As he set me down, I was able to turn back to the mirror, this time to watch my very own boy dance with me.

The next five minutes were wonderfully happy. It seemed impossible that we were still dancing quietly and serenely together when what I wanted to do was laugh and sing, to release the excitement inside me. It seemed impossible not to stop, turn, look this boy who had come into my life full in the face and say hello. But I put off the moment of pleasure until our dance should come to its end. In their training dancers develop a sense of order; each movement and phrase begun must have an end. Our dance together had reached its climax and now it must end as naturally as it had begun.

Then I was conscious of a difference in the boy next to me. I probably would not have noticed it if we had not shared so much together, but his movements became more controlled. I felt that he was planning our next steps instead of improvising joyously as he had done before. I became ill at ease. The couple in the mirror reappeared as strangers again. The boy stopped dancing. The girl stopped too.

*And then I felt the aftermath of his lips on my cheek*

I waited beside him patiently, sure that he would begin
again to create the steps that would allow our dance to end as
beautifully and simply as it had begun. I watched him lean
slowly toward the girl in the mirror and touch her cheek gently
with his lips. He shouldn't do that, I thought. He shouldn't do
that . . . he has not ended our dance. And then I felt the
aftermath of his lips on my cheek. For just a moment it felt
nice and warm, but as I watched the girl in the mirror raise her
hand slowly to her cheek and touch the spot where she had
been kissed, my cheek suddenly became hotter and hotter and
then with an unbearable warmth it spread into my legs. I

couldn't stand on my legs. I knew if I didn't leave the room immediately my legs would no longer support me. I looked just once directly at the boy, my eyes begging him to hold my hand and make me stay, but he seemed too startled by the kiss to understand. Sadly, I knew I would have to provide the ending for our dance. I walked slowly away from the mirror, watching myself and my movements to find the inspiration to end the dance.

I paused for a moment in the doorway and raised my hand slowly to touch my cheek, which still tingled slightly with a sad afterthought. The movement seemed to say good-by. I held the pose for a moment longer as I looked into the mirror to see its effect. The boy sat quietly looking straight ahead. The girl was saying good-by. Our dance had ended.

## Swan Lake

I was just beginning to enjoy my new rank as a soloist with Ballet Theatre when they were forced to disband for a time. As there was only one other ballet company in the United States and I did not want to dance with them, I was a dancer without a place to dance.

I was also a dancer alone in New York City with no money and no job. But I wasn't worried about that. I was worried about dancing the role of Odette, the Queen of the Swans. *Swan Lake* was the first ballet I had ever seen, and I had made it my goal. Each step upward in Ballet Theatre had seemed to bring me closer to my dream, and now all I could think about was that I couldn't dance *Swan Lake*.

*Swan Lake* or not, I had to eat and I took a job with a Broadway show. I hated it but it was good for me. It meant that I could stay in New York and resume my studies. I had lost a lot of technique through missing my daily classes when I was on tour.

While I was with the show Alicia Alonso asked me if I would join her ballet company. Her company's home base was in Havana, Cuba, and she was planning a South American tour. I wasn't sure that I wanted to go on another tour but she mentioned the magic words *Swan Lake* and told me I could be her understudy in the part of Odette. I gave two weeks' notice and bought a pocket Spanish dictionary. I looked up *Swan Lake* in Spanish and was ready for anything South America had to offer.

That continent may have had a great deal to offer but we never had any money in our pockets to find out. After the third week we never got paid because most of the time the South American concert managers did not pay Alicia.

The company paid our hotel bills but sometimes there wasn't enough money even for that and we were locked out of our rooms. There is no feeling like coming ravenously hungry into a hotel dining room and being told you cannot eat because the company has not paid the bill.

One day some of us walked out of the hotel and found our way blocked by three tanks with their guns pointed straight at us. Barbed wire was strewn about and soldiers with guns were all around. We were in the middle of a revolution. When the shooting started we went to the roof of the hotel and not even the bullets flying overhead could make us leave.

On this tour with Alicia I met a young dancer named Nicholas Magallanes. Nicky told me a new company called the New York City Ballet was being formed. I was excited as he spoke about its aims. The founders wanted to develop a new American ballet tradition with young dancers who would be trained in this new tradition by their choreographer, George Balanchine. Nicky said he had worked with Balanchine and that he was a great inspiration.

It was the first time I had heard of anyone interested in developing artistic standards who had the requisite ability and integrity. Nicky was leaving to join the new company and said that if I was ever interested in leaving Alicia's company I should write to him in New York.

After a particularly harrowing plane trip high over the Andes in a plane so old that we could look up at the sky through holes in the fuselage, I made up my mind to leave South America and join the New York City Ballet if they would take me. I wrote a long letter to Nicky to ask if there was a place for me. I told him I didn't have any money for a plane ticket. When I finished the letter, almost in tears, I realized I didn't even have money enough for a stamp. The next day I approached three of my friends and among us we were able to raise the money to buy an air-mail stamp.

A week later an answer came by cable. It said, "Pick up ticket Pan American." There was no other message. The sender's name was George Balanchine.

I landed in New York City and before I looked for a place to live I went to the School of American Ballet, where Mr. Balanchine taught the company. I was anxious to study with this new company which I hoped would be my home. The class was a thrilling experience. I had never been taught by a teacher with Mr. Balanchine's sense of musical phrasing. Each movement took on a new meaning. I learned to accent a step musically, dancing on top of the music instead of through it.

When class was over I wanted to introduce myself to Mr.

Balanchine and thank him for his kindness in sending me my ticket. I looked at him but he only nodded and walked away. I was very disappointed because I thought he hadn't liked the way I danced. I did not know then that, despite his genius and freedom of expression in dance, he is a shy man.

In the next few weeks I was taught the repertoire of the New York City Ballet. Fortunately I learn choreography quickly but there was much to remember. I bought a big notebook and every night after I got home I wrote down each step and each movement I had learned that day. I still have the notebook and whenever I learn a new ballet I write it down. Thus I have an invaluable record of every ballet I have ever danced.

After the rehearsal period was over I danced my first New York season with the New York City Ballet. It was a new experience. In all the other ballets I had danced I was always conscious of steps, and of moving from place to place on stage. With Mr. Balanchine's choreography, once the ballet started all I did was listen to the music. There has never been a joy in my life like feeling my body seem to move by itself to the demands the music made upon it.

It was a wonderful season in another way. The audience accepted me and liked me. The City Center audience is like a family. Once they accept a performer as a member of the family, they are warm and giving, but if they feel a dancer does not belong, they can be very cold.

Only one thing marred an otherwise perfect season. Mr. Balanchine rarely gave me a correction or coached me in a role. I couldn't understand this. He seemed to like my dancing because he kept putting me in more and more of his ballets. Sometimes after a performance he would walk by me, nod his head, and smile. I knew his smile was his way of saying, "Good," but I wished he would say it aloud.

More than words of encouragement, I wanted guidance. I felt that the more I could become a Balanchine dancer, the more I would enjoy dancing and the better dancer I would become.

I used to take every class he gave and study just how he wanted a movement made. I listened to every word of correction he gave to another dancer in the company and thought about how that could apply to me. I hoped that someday he would take the time to work with me individually, but until that time came I would make the most of every opportunity.

A year and then two years went by with the New York City Ballet. I gained more knowledge and audience acceptance. Their applause was warmer and warmer. The critics were beginning to notice me and write glowing reviews. Members of the company would compliment me on my performance and ask my advice about their parts. It seemed to me that the only person who had not completely accepted me was Mr. Balanchine.

It was a puzzling and heartbreaking time for me. I wondered why Mr. Balanchine never offered me any corrections or worked with me in his new ballets. Then Mr. Martin, the dance critic of the New York *Times,* wrote, "Miss Hayden's dancing fairly bursts the seams of Mr. Balanchine's choreography." Mr. Martin meant the review as a compliment but I was distraught. Could it be that youthful attack was still showing through my work? For a while I tried to be more passive on stage but I didn't feel right. It wasn't me. I made up my mind that, much as I loved and respected Mr. Balanchine, I would have to love and respect my own artistic integrity as well. If he felt I was too strong for his choreography I would accept whatever guidance he might offer me or I would learn by watching as I had in the past, but I was accepted in the New York City Ballet as Melissa Hayden and Melissa Hayden I would be.

Shortly after that I was given my first starring role. William Dollar had created a new ballet called *The Duel*. It was about a pagan warrior girl who falls in love with a knight of the Crusades. Not recognizing each other because of their armor, they meet in battle and she is slain by the man she loves. It was the right vehicle for me at the time. In phrasing and dancewise, it was pure attack. I was able to capitalize on my untrained way of dancing, and the freedom I felt transmitted itself to the ballet. I let loose and fairly chewed up the stage with my abandon. The bravos after that opening performance made me cry with happiness. After that the City Center audience seemed to look on me as a kind of favored daughter, a little wild and unruly, but nevertheless loved. I loved them too. They were wonderful.

After *The Duel* it was hard to get back to dancing with controlled feeling. It was difficult but the most invaluable experience I ever had. I made a sharp differentiation in my mind between the style and requirements of each ballet I danced, and the discipline I exerted made me a more rounded performer.

I hoped Mr. Balanchine would recognize this new plateau I had reached and in his way he did. He allowed me to understudy more of his ballets. I learned them by watching other performers from the wings of the stage or standing behind and watching them as they rehearsed with Mr. B, as we called him. Rarely did he give me an actual rehearsal and rarely did I dance my first performance of these ballets until another performer was ill. As soon as I performed a ballet Mr. B scheduled me to dance it often but he never allowed me to dance another new ballet until there was an emergency again.

I got to dance almost all the ballets in the repertory when a series of illnesses and sprained ankles beset the company one season when we were on tour in London.

Dancing in *The Duel* that season in London, I attacked the ballet so hard that I hit myself in the stomach with my elbow and knocked myself out on stage. The conductor was new and didn't realize there was anything wrong when the stage manager lowered the curtain. The music continued while the curtain was down and after about three minutes, during which I was revived with smelling salts, the curtain was raised and I continued the ballet at the point the conductor had reached in the music. Head down, studying the score as he conducted, he did not know anything had been amiss until he read in big headlines the next day: BALLERINA KNOCKS SELF OUT IN SPOT SHE IS SUPPOSED TO DIE.

When we came back to New York I was dancing almost all the ballets in the repertoire. I had long since got used to the idea that Mr. Balanchine's and my artistic relationship was one of distant respect and admiration but I still wanted very much to change that. Dancing *Swan Lake* became uppermost in my mind again. If Mr. B saw that I could handle the classic yet dramatic aspects of this ballet he might work with me and create new ballets for me. I had to do *Swan Lake.*

I spoke to him about dancing the ballet and he said no, it was not my style. He would not allow me to understudy it.

I made up my mind I would dance it. The battle lines of what were to be a six-year struggle were drawn.

I accepted a week of summer dance concerts at Jacobs Pillow only because they wanted me to dance the pas de deux from *Swan Lake.* I was very nervous. Dancing the ballet had become more important to me than just another role. In my nervousness I attacked the role the first night like a jet plane instead of a delicate swan. Antony Tudor, who was teaching there that summer, took me aside the next day and gave me some valuable coaching. My *Swan Lakes* that next week were much better. I was beginning to understand the role.

When I came back to the New York City Ballet I spoke to Mr. Balanchine again about dancing *Swan Lake.* The answer was still no.

I did something then that I rarely do. I acted emotionally, before I gave myself time to think the problem through carefully. I left the New York City Ballet and signed a contract with Ballet Theatre as ballerina of the company. I was going to dance *Swan Lake.*

On tour with Ballet Theatre I loved being the ballerina. I liked seeing my name in bold type alone on the theater marquees. I liked everything about the tour except the ballets I was dancing. Much as I liked seeing my name in lights, I liked Mr. Balanchine's choreography more. I made up my mind that after the tour the prodigal daughter would return to City Center and ask to be taken back. In the meantime there was *Swan Lake* to dance and learn. After five or six performances I felt the role was mine. I understood it and was dancing it well. Then I noticed that whenever I danced *Swan Lake* the other dancers from the company, who were not in the ballet, were watching my performance from the wings of the stage. That is the highest praise any ballerina can receive. I had met the challenge of the Swan Queen.

After the tour I returned to the New York City Ballet. The atmosphere was very cool for a while. I felt as if I was being punished for having left. But after a time I was once again accepted as a loyal member of the company. My love and respect for the company and Mr. B were too great not to be felt and it is hard to stay angry at anyone who loves you sincerely.

Mr. Balanchine and I resumed where we had left off. I wanted to dance *Swan Lake* and he did not want me to. Another two years went by and the company was going on tour to Australia and Japan. After three months in Japan the usual assortment of injuries that are part of the rigors of touring had cut the number of leading dancers in the company to half. I was dancing two and three ballets a night. Exhausted and stiff during the day, I could hardly force myself out of bed, but the moment the music started at night I seemed to find new strength. I danced and enjoyed it.

When we left for Australia I was glad of the three days' rest before we had to perform again. The morning of the first performance in Australia I was sleeping late, trying to get my strength back, when my roommate, the ballet mistress of the company, burst into the room.

"Wake up, Millie," she called, "wake up. You have to rehearse. You have to dance *Swan Lake* at the matinee today."

I was awake immediately. "What happened?" I asked.

"Diana is sick and Allegra doesn't feel she's ready to dance it. This is an emergency."

"Does Mr. Balanchine know?" I asked her.

"How would he know?" she replied. "He's in New York six thousand miles away."

"I won't do it unless he knows," I told Vida. All of a sudden the moment had come when I could dance *Swan Lake* and I didn't want to do it. I wanted Mr. Balanchine to ask me to do it. It was probably because it was early in the morning but I was stubborn. I wanted some acknowledgment of the six years I had longed to dance *Swan Lake* with the company and not been allowed to do it.

Vida said the magic words. "Come on, Millie, the company needs you."

I got out of bed, took a cold shower, and went to the theater. There were only two hours before the performance and the Balanchine version was unfamiliar. I rehearsed until it was almost time for the performance.

When I rushed to my dressing room it was filled with my friends. I had fifteen minutes to get into my costume and put on the white body make-up the Swan Queen wears. The costume didn't fit me, so while I put on my make-up the wardrobe woman sewed me into my costume. Vida and two friends were dabbing white make-up on my back and shoulders.

Where are the nerves? I thought calmly as I put on my eye shadow amidst all the busy hands around me. I feel too calm. I feel too icy calm. Something's going to happen. I started to walk to the stage, scarcely hearing the words of good luck that followed me.

Suddenly my knees started to shake, my forehead began to perspire, my stomach felt sick. The reaction I was afraid of had set in.

No, I thought, I won't allow it. I'll stand here in the wings and will myself to dance. I'll concentrate on the ballet. I could hear the audience restlessly waiting for the house lights to dim. This was a familiar sound. I was beginning to feel better. Then there was a silence. I heard applause and knew the conductor had taken his place before the orchestra. The lovely introduction to *Swan Lake* was about to begin.

Now, I said to myself, concentrate on the ballet. Get into the mood of the work. I looked out onto the stage and imagined the mysterious clearing in the middle of the big forest. In the background were the rippling waters of the lake and in the distance was the towering castle of the evil magician, Von Rotbart.

The curtain went up. The stage hands set in motion the mechanical swans that float across the lake during the overture. I saw real swans. I, their Queen, Odette, was leading them, a jeweled crown on my head. In the story these swans are enchanted maidens under the evil spell of Von Rotbart. The lake they float on is made from the tears of my mother. By day we

*Stage hands set in motion the mechanical swans that float across the lake during the overture*

must fly as swans through the sky, but from dusk to dawn we return as maidens to the enchanted clearing. Only if I meet a prince who has never vowed his love to another and who will love me forever can I and the maidens be saved from this dreadful spell.

A group of hunters carrying crossbows accidentally comes to the enchanted clearing. They are searching for the swans they have just seen flying overhead. Their leader, the young and handsome Prince Siegfried, joins them and tells his friends that he wishes to be alone. Prince Siegfried stays behind as the other hunters go off into the forest to find the swans that have suddenly disappeared.

It is time for my entrance. You don't have to think about dancing, I told myself. Don't think about steps. Just tell yourself the story of *Swan Lake*. The dancing will take care of itself.

I am Odette, the Queen of the Swans, I begin. . . .

## The Story

I land in the enchanted clearing and smooth my feathers after my long flight. Sundown is always the saddest moment of the day for me, for as I change from swan to maiden I yearn to be free, to be just a young girl again. How wonderful it would be if a charming prince were to step from behind those trees, pledge his love, and free me from this evil spell. My fluttering swan movements become more womanly as dusk approaches.

Suddenly a man carrying a crossbow steps into the clearing. Gone are all thoughts of princes and freedom. I am afraid. Trembling, I try to escape but it is dusk and I can no longer fly. Tenderly he comforts me and gently places his crossbow at my feet. I look at him timidly for the first time. He is handsome —and he is a prince. I am no longer afraid. I am hopeful as I tell him about the evil spell of Von Rotbart and of the only way I can be saved. But now I have a different fear. Will he love me? Am I beautiful enough?

He seems to want to say something—but there is Von Rotbart, clad in armor, his batlike figure casting eerie shadows on the darkened lake. The prince grabs his crossbow and aims.

Yet he must not shoot, for anyone who tries to kill Von Rotbart will die immediately. Without thought of my own danger, I rush in front of his crossbow and place myself between the prince and Von Rotbart. As I do, I know that I truly love my handsome prince.

Von Rotbart commands me to leave and I must obey. I walk sadly away, hoping all the while that my prince will say the words of love that will set me free and allow me to go with him from these woods which are my prison. But he does not speak. Looking back, I see him leave the clearing and all hope dies.

My friends have been following me and soon appear overhead. With much effort I remember that I am Odette, their

*Without thought of my own danger I rush in front of his crossbow*

Queen, and that I must return to the clearing to see that they are safe for the night. Though my heart is broken, I must be there to comfort them. As they change from swans to maidens, they, too, are very sad and often cry.

I enter the clearing not a moment too soon. My friends have landed and are huddled in a corner, frightened by the hunters, who are aiming crossbows at them. Without hesitation, I rush in front of them and shield them with my body from the hunters' arrows. At this moment I am unafraid because I am a Queen and my serenity causes the hunters to hesitate. At this moment the Prince returns and commands them never to shoot again in this clearing. As a Queen, I thank the prince for saving my subjects and proudly, saying no more, bow in gratitude and walk away. The prince starts to follow but I hurry from him, afraid to trust myself to speak. It would be far worse than Von Rotbart's evil spell to compel the prince to say he loves me because he is sorry for me.

From off in the woods I watch my friends gaily enjoying their visitors. As the evening wears on, I see true love and friendship begin to grow between my friends and the hunters. How lovely they look to me as they sit and talk, their young love shining from their eyes and blending with the moonlight that lights the lake. And how cruel fate is, that they should love and be loved—and for naught—while, if I were loved, all our loves would be fulfilled!

Soon the prince returns to the clearing, looking for someone. One by one, I watch each hunter shake his head no. The Prince must be looking for me. I rush back to the clearing and curtsy deeply at his feet. Gently he lifts me and each tender gesture is an unspoken vow of love. Lost in each other, we fail to notice that there is a faint hint of light in the east, and unless he speaks of his love before the sun touches the horizon, it will be too late. We are both so overcome with the wonders of each

*I watch my friends gaily enjoying their visitors*

other that the outside is no longer with us. A thousand times and with a thousand movements and touches we vow our undying love and faith. Our love is so eloquent that it seems to speak—but never a sound do we utter.

A harsh light blinds our eyes. The sun has broken the horizon and ends our love as it begins its day. Von Rotbart returns and the beating of wings and the rushing of air cause me to look for my friends. I see that they have become swans again, but I have not changed, and for a moment it seems that even our unspoken love is powerful enough to triumph over the spell. My whole body is tortured as the magic of evil pulls at me to become a swan while the beauty of love still holds me as

*A thousand times with a thousand movements and touches we vow our undying love and faith*

a woman. Time after time I rush to hold my prince and too late, too late we say we love, we love. Time after time we are cruelly separated as I am drawn by the beating wings into the mass of swans.

Von Rotbart's magic begins to triumph and slowly I feel myself becoming a swan again. I kiss my Prince for the last time and gently lower his head so that his downcast eyes will have seen me last as a young girl. My tears mingle with those of my mother's in the lake as I become once again Odette, the Queen of the Swans.

*I kiss my prince for the last time*

# Orpheus and Eurydice

When the curtain fell on my performance of *Swan Lake* in Australia many of my friends, who knew how much the ballet meant to me, were crying. I stood in the middle of the stage with tears running down my face for the joy I felt in their love. After many years of working together a ballet company becomes like a family. Like brothers and sisters, we fight, perhaps more than most because we live and work so closely together, but we always feel a loyalty and love for one another. We help each other through difficult times and rejoice together in our moments of triumph.

Perhaps we have this feeling of closeness because we are so shut off from friends on the outside. In high school, serious ballet students have no time for dances, or dates, or school clubs. Immediately after school they rush off to ballet class and spend the rest of the afternoon practicing. Evenings are for homework and rest. There are no summer vacations. The years from twelve to sixteen are critical in a young ballet student's life and she must keep studying during the summer to develop her technique. If she is taken into a ballet company the isolation is more complete. Touring takes her away from home and she loses touch with whatever friends she may have had. She cannot go to college and she has little time to read books or become interested in anything other than ballet class, rehearsal, and performance.

Most of the younger dancers in a company resemble fragile hothouse flowers that have never been exposed to the wind and rain. Because they are so sheltered, their personalities do not develop until later and they are uncomfortable outside of their own environment.

When I attend a party given for the company I watch the younger girls sitting together, scarcely talking to the guests from outside the company, nervous when they are spoken to. I sometimes forget that I was the same way and worry about how much these younger members of the company are giving up because of their dedication to ballet. But it isn't so. Their dedication places them among the lucky few who have found a joy in work and a means of expression. It allows them, when they have mastered the difficult beginnings of ballet, to look about and enjoy other facets of life with the same enthusiasm and devotion that they give to their work. This blooming comes later in life than it does for most people but it is more complete and rewarding because dancers have been trained to commit themselves fully to everything they do.

Perhaps the loneliest part of being a dancer is the difficulty of starting a family of your own. Dancers marry later than most women. It is hard to meet young men and most husbands do not relish the idea of having a wife who is always away from home at rehearsals and performances. I am very lucky, for I have a wonderful husband and two lovely children, a son Stuart, and a daughter Jennifer.

Until I met my husband, Don Coleman, I thought I might not marry. I wanted to very much but none of the men I met would accept me as I was. Many of them wanted me to give up dancing. I could never have done that no matter how much I loved anyone. As Don said when he asked me to marry him, "Dancing is a part of you as you are. If you gave it up, you would be a different person. I love you. I might not love that different person."

Don was the stage manager of the company and we had a traveling courtship. He proposed to me in Buffalo and I said yes in Memphis, Tennessee. We got our marriage license in Ruston, Louisiana, and were married in New Orleans.

We were performing at the Louisiana Technical College in Ruston and the dean of students helped us get our marriage license. We hadn't told anyone in the company we were going to be married and we swore the dean to secrecy. He was thrilled to have a part of our secret romance.

We had to wait three days after the issuance of the license, by which time we were in New Orleans, a beautifully romantic city, just perfect for a wedding. The French Quarter has lovely old houses with filigreed latticework and vines growing up to flower-covered balconies. We went to the courthouse in the French Quarter and chose the first judge whose name we saw on the directory. We walked up a long flight of curving marble stairs to the office and found that we had chosen the only female judge in New Orleans. She was a charming woman with bright red hair—very Southern and very female. She cried when Don put the ring on my finger and kissed me. Our witnesses were the ballet master and the wardrobe mistress of the company. We had sworn them to secrecy too because we didn't want anyone to know we were married until we had a chance to write to our parents.

After the ceremony we went to a French restaurant and sat down to a New Orleans wedding breakfast with chilled champagne. The ballet master drank toast after toast to the bride and groom. When the party was over I went to a two o'clock rehearsal and Don went to the theater to supervise the stage crew who were hanging the scenery. We made a great effort to appear unconcerned but it was no use. People began coming up to congratulate us. The ballet master had drunk too much champagne and had given away our secret.

Even though the rest of the tour was very difficult, it was a honeymoon to us. We went next to Dallas, Texas, where the company had a party for us, and then to Los Angeles and San Francisco. From there we traveled to Seattle and Vancouver, British Columbia. Then the company started working its way back home across the northern part of the United States. Both Don and I love to travel and we enjoyed waking up in a different city every morning.

When we got back I stopped dancing to wait for the birth of our first child, Stuart. I missed dancing very much but I enjoyed being just a wife. We went apartment hunting and found a very nice one overlooking the East River. I shopped for furniture and entered on my life of domesticity with the same enthusiasm I feel for dancing. I have always been an excellent cook and it was fun to cook meals for my husband and invite guests for dinner. I have never minded criticism from dance critics but with my cooking it was different. If dinner guests did not rave about my food and eat at least two helpings I felt grumpy and neglected.

I took my first ballet class one month after Stuart was born. It was hard to resume classes because I wanted so much just

*I took my first ballet class one month after Stuart was born*

to stay home and hold my baby and love him but I knew that I must begin again. Although dancing was no longer my whole life, it was a part of my life that I could not do without. The fact that I could love so many things made me a better mother, a better wife, and a better dancer. The only terrible wrench I felt was when I had to go away on tour. I hated to leave my child and I felt I was being unfair to him. A mother should be at home with her children.

However, young as he was, I think Stuart understood. From the age of two he loved to watch performances. He would sit in the wings off stage, legs crossed on the floor, solemnly watching all that was going on. At first I used to worry for fear he might walk out onto the stage but he seemed to know instinctively that he was not to do this. When he heard the audience applaud, he would quietly clap his little hands together. After a while he began to applaud at the places he liked whether the audience applauded or not. He began to appreciate me in a role other than that of his mother just as I was beginning to respect him as a little individual as well as my son.

When I was away he could visualize what I was doing and I think this made the parting less difficult for him. I wrote him long letters telling him everything I did each day and his father read them to him. The parting was made easier for my by the letters Don wrote me about Stuart. He told me in detail everything Stuart did from the moment he woke in the morning till he went to bed at night. When I left for Australia, Stuart was only three and a half years old and if it hadn't been for Don's letters I would have missed three of the most beautiful months of my son's growing up.

As Stuart grew older I used to tell him the stories of the ballets before he went to a performance. For a long time his favorite was *Swan Lake* and he saw almost every matinee performance I danced. After a while his taste broadened and began to include all the story ballets. Once he was very disappointed in me. He was going to see a performance of *Orpheus and Eurydice* and he asked me to tell him the story first. In that ballet I dance the part of Eurydice and I am on the stage for only a short time, when I dance a short pas de deux with Orpheus, who is really the main character of the ballet and about whom all the action is centered. I told Stuart the story very sketchily because I had really concerned myself only with the time I was on stage. After the ballet was over he came back to my dressing room with his face filled with questions.

"Mommy," he asked, "why are all those people carrying rocks?"

"I don't know," I said.

"But why were those women angry at Orpheus?"

"Maybe they didn't like him," I said weakly.

His expression clearly told me I had let him down.

The next day I went to a bookstore and bought a book on Greek mythology. Stuart and I spent many long pleasant hours together reading the story of the Greek myths. I enjoyed them quite as much as he. I read him the story of Orpheus and Eurydice and I was flattered and delighted when he said, "It's very good but I like your stories better. Tell me the ballet story of *Orpheus and Eurydice* the way you tell me the other ballet stories."

"Give me a little time," I said, "to think about the story. I'll tell it to you tomorrow when you come home from school and are eating your lunch." I worked harder preparing that story than on that of any other ballet I have danced.

The next day Stuart came home from school, rushed into the house, kissed me, and said, "Now tell me the story."

"But you must keep eating," I said as I began to tell him my version of *Orpheus and Eurydice*.

## The Story

The banks of the river Styx are always still. The wind comes here seldom and blows without sound. The cricket does not chirp nor does the grasshopper make the slightest scratch as he rubs his legs together.

The banks of this river separate my husband Orpheus and me from the world above. We live in the lower world now, which is the name we Greeks give to the place where we go when our lives on earth are over.

My name is Eurydice. When Orpheus and I were first married we lived above in the land of Greece. We were very happy there until one day, while I was walking through the fields, I was bitten on the heel by a serpent and was taken to the lower world.

From the lower world we are able to see our loved ones above and I was very saddened to watch Orpheus. He was so anguished that he searched throughout the land to find the river Styx so that he might join me.

Wherever he went, he played the lyre which his father Apollo, the god of music, had given him. He sang of the tragedy that had befallen us and all who heard his song cried and were saddened, but no man could lead him to the banks of the river Styx and to the cave that is the entrance to the lower world.

*I was very saddened to watch Orpheus*

Pluto and Proserpine, who are the rulers of the lower world, heard Orpheus' song. They were so moved by the beauty of his music that they decided to permit him to visit them. They told me that if, on seeing him, they should judge him to be as worthy as his song they would permit me to return to Greece with him and live out my life till its natural end. I was happy but fearful for Orpheus because Pluto and Proserpine had never before permitted anyone to leave their kingdom.

Each mortal has a ghostly spirit, called a Dark Messenger, who lives below and is united with him when his life on earth has ended. Pluto and Proserpine summoned Orpheus' Dark Messenger and instructed him to bring Orpheus before them.

The Dark Messenger set forth and found Orpheus in the countryside playing his lyre and woefully singing his song. The woodland creatures sat at his feet listening quietly, and even the lions and tigers of the forest had gathered about him, enraptured by the enchanted sound. The rocks and boulders along the roadside had moved nearer to the sound of the music and grew softer and cried as the notes floated sadly about their heads.

The Dark Messenger fastened a golden mask over Orpheus' eyes, took the lyre from him, and began to play. He told Orpheus in song of the conditions of the journey. Orpheus was to travel with him to the thrones of Pluto and Proserpine where all the creatures of the underworld would be gathered. There he was to play his lyre and sing for them. If his music charmed each and every spirit that dwelled there, then Orpheus would be permitted to leave with me for the upper world. But he was never to remove the golden mask until he reached the upper world again.

As the Dark Messenger strummed the lyre the banks of the river Styx sprang up all about them. This river had never been more than a step away from Orpheus wherever he went in all his travels, flowing invisibly by him as it flows unseen by every mortal man. No searching can ever find it and yet, when it finally appears, it must be crossed. The stern ferryman who guards the banks of the river was waiting. They stepped into his boat and were quickly ferried to the entrance of the cave, which is guarded by Cerberus, a three-headed dog with hair of snakes. No two heads of the dog ever sleep at one time. He has been a constant sentinel at this eternal portal since the beginning of time.

Orpheus followed the sound of his lyre past Cerberus and down through the steep and winding passages that led to the center of the earth and the thrones of Pluto and Proserpine.

When they arrived, the Dark Messenger stopped playing and Orpheus stood quietly waiting for his lyre to be placed in his hand. All the creatures of the underworld were gathered about him but no one ceased his task or even noted his presence by the slightest pause.

The stern furies were there, busy with their uncompromising duty of meting out punishment to those whose crimes were not within the reach of human justice. No plea for mercy has ever been known to move them.

Ixion, the King of Thessaly, was present, chained by serpents to a wheel that constantly turned, blown by a strong wind.

Up a steep hill Sisyphus, the King of Corinth, unendingly pushed his heavy stone only to have it roll down each time he tortuously reached the top.

There, too, was Tantalus, constantly maddened by thirst as he stood up to his neck in water, which receded as he continuously tried to drink.

These and countless more were Orpheus' unseen audience.

The air was heavy with the unending sound of the slow movements of those who may never cease their efforts or know the joy of pausing and regarding their completed work.

Orpheus' task began. His spirit played the lyre and the music was more beauteous than had ever before been heard. Then Orpheus strummed the lyre with such feeling and love that each note sang like the voices of a thousand angels yet no one was distracted from his eternal task. Many times Orpheus thought he had failed and could not go on but each time his spirit snatched the lyre from his hand and continued to play. Back and forth passed the lyre with never a note missed and the music growing in tenderness and love. Finally Orpheus took the lyre and caressed the strings with all the love and beauty we felt for each other. The voices of the thousand angels came together as one voice. Each note sang so full that the huge cave was filled with a loveliness that left no room for pain or suffering.

A tear came into the eyes of one of the furies and soon all the furies were crying unashamedly. Sisyphus sat quietly on his rock and Ixion's wheel became still. Even Tantalus ceased for a moment his efforts to drink. For the first time since the gods created the underworld, all was still. The sounds of suffering which had continued since the beginning of the world were silenced. Then and only then did the Dark Messenger take the lyre from Orpheus and permit him to stop playing. Orpheus stood quietly, his head bowed, waiting for the verdict. The golden mask covered his eyes. In the complete silence his ears strained for any sound of the outcome.

Pluto and Proserpine nodded silently to the Dark Messenger and I was brought into the presence of my husband. It only remained for us to make the long journey to the mouth of the cave and we would be reunited. I longed to run and hold my husband but it was necessary to show the same fortitude as he. His courage became mine and with strength and dignity I quietly bowed good-by to Pluto and Proserpine and their subjects. Although I wanted above all else to go with my husband, I was sad to leave. Since I had done no evil on earth, my life below had been filled with many pleasures and kindnesses.

I called to my husband that I was ready for our journey. The sound of my words shattered the silence and all the creatures stirred slightly from the trance the music had placed them in but Orpheus did not move. I had a premonition of fear as I realized that I was still a part of the underworld and that he could not hear me until we reached the other bank of the river Styx. Hopefully I placed my hand in his but I knew what the outcome would be. He could not feel my touch. I placed my cheek tenderly on his shoulder and although he seemed for just a moment to be aware of my nearness, he could not know I was with him.

The Dark Messenger began to play the lyre again and move upward to the sun. As the sounds of the strings began to move away, Orpheus knew he was to follow.

My heart ached to reassure him as we walked along. To have come so far and to leave without knowing whether I were with him must be a task too difficult for any man. I hoped the strength of my love would give him courage to go on but he was unaware of my presence. He walked with such sadness and yet with such fortitude that I was aware of him as the son of a god as well as my husband.

*My heart ached to reassure him*

*I hoped the strength of my love would give him courage*

The ground began to level beneath our feet and we both
knew that we would soon come to the entrance of the cave. I
felt my husband's steps grow slower and hesitate and I knew
I must reassure him in some way that I was with him. I walked
around him and held his face in my hands. I willed my entire
soul to give strength to my fingers that cupped his cheek so
that they would convey my love and my presence through their
touch. I summoned all my powers and Orpheus knew. He knew
I was with him. His happiness was so intense that all else was
forgotten and he ripped the golden mask from his eyes so that
he could behold me. I tried to look into the eyes of my husband

but immediately a deep white mist sprang up about me. As I
was drawn into its eerie whiteness, I remembered the last time
I had seen that same mist. It was when I was bitten by the
serpent.

I looked hopefully for my husband but I was not surprised
when the face of my Dark Messenger appeared through the
mist and took me kindly by the hand.

I watched Orpheus once again from below as he stood by the
still river's bank and then the river disappeared and he was
left forlorn and alone in the countryside. As if in a dream he
plucked at the strings of his lyre. The music moaned like the
sound of the winter wind chilling the leafless boughs of the
trees. The rocks and boulders shivered with the cold of the
sound while the lions and tigers slunk off into the forest and
huddled about their cubs to give them warmth. Orpheus was
alone. He wandered like that for many days till one day he
came upon a wild band of Thracian women. They called to
Orpheus to join them but he was too dazed to see them and the
sound of his music drowned out their voices. They did not
understand this and thought Orpheus was ignoring them, which
infuriated them. One of them became so angry that she hurled
her javelin at Orpheus, but as soon as the javelin came within
the sound of his music it became charmed and fell harmlessly
to the ground. This angered the women even more and they
fell into such a state of fury that they all hurled their javelins
at Orpheus. Each javelin, one by one, stopped and lay quietly
at his feet as the music calmed their swift flight. The women
became so frenzied that they began hurling rocks at him and
screaming insults at Orpheus. Their screams drowned out the
sound of his music and the rocks soon reached him and left him
senseless on the ground. Wildly the women tore him limb from
limb and threw his heart and lyre into the river Hebrus. Wherever his heart and lyre floated down the stream, along the banks

*A wild band of Thracian women*

*Wildly the women tore him limb from limb*

was heard the ghostly murmur of their sad music. The muses gathered his body and buried it at Libertha where, it is said, the lark sings the sweetest in all the world.

The Dark Messenger came for Orpheus and once again they crossed the river Styx. This time Orpheus and I were united forever.

The gods were so saddened that they took his lyre and placed it among the stars in the sky. All who love music may see it there, in the still of night, and play melodies on it in their hearts.

# Still Point

Generally speaking, my life in the New York City Ballet follows a concentrated routine of study and performance.

I wake in the morning at nine o'clock, do my chores about the house, and then go to the School of American Ballet where I take the eleven o'clock morning professional class. Afternoons are spent with my children or at rehearsal if I am scheduled. On performance days I go to the theater about five-thirty in the evening, put on my make-up, and do a slow careful barre to make sure my body is properly warmed up for the performance. The rest of my time before the curtain goes up is spent in going over difficult sections of the ballet I will dance that evening. Since we are a repertory company, I have danced the ballet I am going to perform many times before and my only challenge is to maintain my own standards of performance or try to improve the places where I am not satisfied with myself.

This quiet, well-ordered regularity is necessary for any serious ballet company and Mr. Balanchine, who is the artistic director and choreographer of the company, sees that it is maintained.

Mr. B and Lincoln Kirstein founded the New York City Ballet. As a young man Lincoln Kirstein was very interested in ballet and his dream was to have an American ballet company that would create an American tradition of dance.

In order to do this, he had to find a choreographer who had

the ability and inclination to start afresh, training young dancers and building a new company.

By all past indications, this should have been an impossible task. In the entire history of ballet, which is more than four hundred years old, the great choreographers can be counted on the fingers of one hand. Part of the reason lies in the restrictions that ballet has placed upon itself. Ballet began in France as part of the royal entertainment at the court of the King. Its primary function was to present the human body in its most beautiful and aristocratic manner. To that end, any step or movement that did not present the dancer in her most flattering line was rejected. Over the course of the years only about thirty permissible steps or movements have remained, each with a name and each to be danced in an exact, prescribed manner. Ballet is the only dance form with a precise number of codified steps and, though it has achieved its purpose of being the most beautiful form of dance, it is also the most limited.

Not only must a choregrapher have the imagination and invention to know how to combine these few movements into original dance but he must contain these movements within the restrictions of the music he has chosen for his ballet. He must work with groups of dancers, moving them on the stage in interesting and clear patterns. It is small wonder that there have been so few choreographers of true genius throughout the history of ballet.

I like to think fate determined that while Lincoln Kirstein was having his dream in America, unknown to him a sixteen-year-old dancer and choreographer named George Balanchine was about to leave Russia because he had no opportunity to create the new work in ballet that he envisioned.

Balanchine was born in Russia, the son of a musician and composer. When he was five years old his mother arranged for him to take piano lessons. He not only learned to play the piano, he studied theory and harmony. He was an eager pupil and soon became an excellent pianist with a sound knowledge of musical theory.

When he was nine years old his parents took his sister to apply for admission to the Imperial School of Ballet. George went with them and was left in the waiting room while his sister was auditioned. There is no equivalent to the Imperial Ballet School anywhere in the world. Young children from all over Russia apply for admission each year. Rigid examinations are held. The first test is physical appearance. Legs must be long, torsos straight and in perfect proportion, and the face must be either handsome or have a kind of character that will project well from the stage. Only those children with perfect dancers' bodies pass the first requirement. No child is admitted to the school unless the examining board feels he is a potential member of the ballet company.

The applicants who pass the first test are then subjected to more exhaustive tests to see whether they have the talent for ballet. Musical aptitude, feeling for movement, and self-discipline are necessary for success at the school. Discipline is essential at the Imperial School, for the children who are accepted live at the school night and day for eight years. Their daily curriculum consists of academic schoolwork, dance classes, music classes, and classes in pantomime, character dancing, and make-up. The entire day is spent in study. When a student completes his term of study at the school he is eligible for membership in the Imperial Ballet Company.

George Balanchine's sister was not accepted, but while he was waiting patiently for the results of her audition he was taken into another room with six other boys. He was told to walk around. Then he was sent to still another room where he was examined further. He was still confused by the attention that had been paid him when he was told by his mother that he had been accepted at the school and that he was to stay there for eight years. That same day his parents left George in the strange surroundings and went home.

Lonesome and distraught, the boy ran away to find an aunt who lived in St. Petersburg. He was found by the police and returned to the school. After a time the pain of the separation from his parents grew dim and George began to apply himself to his work. He was not tall enough to be a great classical dancer but he began to develop a perfect technique and the strength he developed in the execution of steps was phenomenal. This came in large part from his insistence that he understand the reason why each step was done in a certain way and what muscles of the body controlled each movement. When class was over he would go off by himself and think through the entire class. He knew which steps at the barre were designed to improve the dancer's jump and which steps were important to develop balance. He never accepted anything that was said in class without questioning it to himself after class and understanding why. He watched the great teachers at the school coach the principal dancers of the company and made a mental note of what points they stressed. He began to be interested not in dance so much as in the construction of dance.

When Mr. B was fifteen years old he formed a group from among the students at the Imperial School and choreographed ballets for them. The students competed to see who would be allowed to place their free time at the disposal of this young boy who told them how and when to move.

For a long time, even though he was interested in his work at the school, his first love was music and while still at the school he applied for admission to the state Conservatory of Music. He was examined by the leading composers and musicians in Russia on both his talent as a pianist and his theoretical knowledge of music. He was granted a scholarship at the conservatory and attended classes there along with his work at the Imperial School.

Upon graduating from the Imperial School, Mr. B became a member of the corps de ballet of the St. Petersburg Ballet Company, while at the same time continuing his musical studies at the conservatory. Despite his demonstrated ability as a choreographer he was given little opportunity to work in that capacity. The company was rigid with tradition and the older choreographers would not allow room for so young and talented a rival.

In recognition of his exceptional talent he was given permission to form a small group of dancers from the company and leave Russia to tour Europe with them. He took his group to Europe and never returned to Russia. He was determined to do what he loved most—choreography.

He spent four years in Paris, working very little and often hungry, and then he was discovered by the great ballet impresario Diaghilev and became a part of the Ballets Russes. At twenty-one Balanchine became ballet master of the company and began to create ballets that are still danced today.

At the same time Lincoln Kirstein was in Europe searching for a choreographer and teacher who would be able to form an American company. Kirstein had been at his task for many years, had seen many choreographers, and was discouraged about ever finding anyone with the ability he envisioned. He was dubious when his European friends told him he must see the young choreographer at the Ballets Russes. More out of duty than hope, he went to see the company. After watching his first Balanchine ballet he knew his search was over. His only fear was that he would not be able to convince the young man that he should come to America.

Kirstein knew that Balanchine not only had complete freedom to do the kind of ballets he wanted but was inspired by the host of talent which surrounded Diaghilev at all times. Diaghilev had the happy faculty of recognizing and attracting to himself the greatest creative artists in the world. While Balanchine was with Diaghilev he influenced and was influenced by such great men as Stravinsky, Rieti, Auric, Utrillo, Matisse, and many others.

But despite all this, Kirstein's offer to Balanchine to come to America fell on receptive ears. Balanchine knew that European audiences, steeped in a four-hundred-year-old history of ballet, were more used to spectacle on the stage than to dance and were more concerned with the story of princes and enchanted maidens than with seeing movement danced for its own beauty. Europe regarded ballet as traditional and Balanchine knew there is nothing harder to change than habit that is dignified by the solemn word "tradition." Balanchine was anxious to come to America where he and the audiences could mature together.

Balanchine's and Kirstein's first step was to form the School of American Ballet. They gathered together the best ballet teachers for the faculty and established the school on the same principles as those of the Imperial School in Russia. To this day no student is accepted for training at the School of American Ballet unless he or she is seriously interested in ballet as a career and has the potential to become a part of the New York City Ballet. Today almost all the members of the New York City Ballet are products of the school that Balanchine and Kirstein formed nearly thirty years ago.

At the same time that Balanchine and Kirstein formed their ballet school they formed a small ballet company called the American Ballet. Their first season was only two weeks long but those who saw the company perform were most impressed. Soon the company became the resident company at the Metropolitan Opera House, giving it a stable base on which to grow.

It soon outgrew the restriction inherent in being an opera ballet company and left the Met, eventually becoming the New York City Ballet, which has toured the entire world and performs in New York City for more than twenty weeks a year.

Mr. Balanchine and other choreographers create many new ballets for the New York City Ballet each year. My greatest satisfaction as a dancer is working with these choreographers while a new ballet is being originated. When I am called for rehearsal I try to remove from my mind all preconceived thoughts about the music and subject matter of the new ballet. Often a choreographer first imagines movement in his mind but he must see the movement performed by a dancer before he knows whether it is really what he wants. I try to make myself the complete tool of the choreographer and re-create faithfully the movement he wishes to see.

When I was learning *Medea* I was working with a Swedish choreographer named Birgit Cullberg. At the same time, Judith Anderson was appearing in the theatrical version of *Medea* on television. It was a great temptation to watch her performance. I knew there was a great deal I could learn from her about the dramatic content of *Medea*. But ballet and theater are two different mediums and Miss Cullberg, who created with movement, would have to see the role differently than an author who created with words. If I had seen Miss Anderson's work before the ballet was completed it would have been impossible for me not to let her influence me during rehearsal and I would have been unable to give Miss Cullberg the freedom she needed to do her work. Only after all the steps were set did I begin to add my interpretation to the role. But by then the framework was complete and I was governed by the steps the choreographer had created.

When I work with Mr. Balanchine I find it important not to form any preconceived idea of the music before the ballet

*Rehearsing with Mr. B*

is completely finished. Mr. B's extraordinary talent lies not only in his invention of movement but in the way he phrases the movement to fit his interpretation of the musical phrasing. No two people receive the same values from music. If I thought about the music before a rehearsal, I would never be as pliable as when I learn the steps simultaneously with hearing the music. When the ballet is completed, I go home and listen to the music, if it has been recorded, over and over. But as I hear the music I remember the steps and phrasing and the two become fused.

An exception to my rule was when I first learned and premièred the ballet *Still Point* with the New York City Ballet. Its choreographer, Todd Bolender, had originated the ballet with another company and before he began teaching me the steps he asked me to watch the other company's performance of the ballet. At first I thought the ballet was not for me. One of my pet peeves with dramatic ballets is that the dancer usually feels that dance is not as powerful as the spoken word and that she must overact to get her point across to the audience. Most of the dramatic acting I have seen in dance tends to be melodramatic and unbelievable to me. At first viewing *Still Point* seemed much too much the story of an emotional woman who was out of touch with the world about her. I can't dance that kind of role. I must be able to ground every action on stage to a reality of feeling somewhere in my own experience.

I was very unhappy as I began rehearsals with Todd. I learned the steps but dreaded the moment when the ballet would be complete and I would have to dance it straight through, adding myself to the movements of the ballet.

Finally the time was drawing close and I tried to shut out of my mind the preconceived notion I had about the interpretation. I knew that the central theme of the ballet was loneliness but after I grew up I never experienced the extreme loneliness I had felt as a young girl. What, I thought, if I try to make my characterization that of a young girl who is experiencing the first pain of entering the adult world? That way I could soften the harsh dramatic qualities I objected to when I saw the ballet, yet I could still say everything the choreographer intended.

I have never asked Todd whether he is happy with my story of *Still Point* but I love the ballet now, because there is so much of me in the young sixteen-year-old girl and her lonely walk toward womanhood.

## The Story

As I walked down the street I felt lonely. I grew up with two girl friends and we had always been together. But lately I had seen less and less of them and since my sweet-sixteen party the week before I had not seen them at all. They were very strange at the party. Everyone was having a good time but they seemed bored. I called them on the telephone but they weren't in. Their mothers said they had gone to the library to study but when I went to look for them they weren't there.

Walking down the street, I made up my mind to find them and ask them if they were angry.

I came to the park where we used to watch the older boys and girls walking, holding hands, or sitting together on the grass. Some of the couples waved and I recognized them as my classmates. I was an "older girl" now but I didn't feel like one.

I wished I could sit in the park and enjoy talking to a boy the way they did. Every time a boy spoke to me, I felt very shy and could think of nothing to say.

Off in the distance I saw two couples sitting together on the grass. They seemed to be enjoying themselves so much that I envied them. As I came closer I realized that they were my friends and two of the boys from our class. Before I could stop myself, I was running across the grass to them with a carefree

*I grew up with two girl friends and we were always together*

expression on my face. It was forced and as I ran I wished I could walk up to them as my natural self. "Hi!" I said to them, my voice sounding shrill to my ears. "I'm glad I found you."

They introduced me to the two boys and then no one said anything. I stayed quiet as long as I could and then I began to chatter nervously to my friends about school, about dresses, about all the things we used to talk of when we were alone. I knew I was ignoring the boys and I wanted to say something to them but I couldn't think of anything to say.

My friends were interested in what I was saying. They seemed to forget about the boys and be happy that we were together again. I realized that they were uncomfortable with boys too. I wondered if all the girls in our class who seemed to get along with boys so well might not feel the same way but knew how to hide it better than I did.

"Come on, let's go," I heard one of the boys say.

"Yeah," said the other boy. "If you three want to have a little girls' conversation you don't need us."

"Oh no!" my girl friend said. "Stay." And they both looked at me as if I were a complete stranger.

They ignored me and began talking to the boys. I stood tense. My head turned as I looked interestedly at each person who spoke, hoping for some recognition from them.

The boys were doing most of the talking. They spoke about the basketball game at high school and the latest records. I kept thinking it wasn't much different from what they had called the little-girl conversation but still I could find no way either to leave them or to be with them.

I saw one of the boys whisper to my friends, who shook their heads. The boy was more insistent. I turned my head away so they wouldn't think I was eavesdropping. One of my friends called my name and my head moved quickly to look at her.

"We're leaving now. Don't you have to go home and study?" She couldn't hold my eyes when she said this to me. Before I could think of anything to say they all started to walk away.

I stood where I was, alone. Before, I had felt lonely but now loneliness was a part of me. As I stood there feeling sorry for myself I began to have a new feeling. I was experiencing myself . . . alone. I had never thought of myself as just me before. It was always my parents and I or my friends and I or my teachers and I. I began to like myself just as I was. There was no need to pretend I was someone I wasn't. I didn't have to apologize for liking classical music and books.

I closed my eyes to shut out everything except the delicious

*Before, I had felt lonely but now loneliness was a part of me*

feeling I was beginning to have about myself. When I opened them everything about me was the same. I was surprised because I felt so different. I felt so quiet and still. I felt grown up. I *was* an "older girl" now.

I saw that my friends and the boys had stopped farther down the path and were arguing. They began walking toward me. I wondered what they wanted.

I said, "Hello!" Before, I would have put on an eager expression. Thank goodness that pretending was over.

"Come on," the boys said, "you can come with us. We're going to take a walk behind the baseball diamond. We'll get a friend for you and you'll be his girl."

"No," I said, "I want to go home now." I understood why

my friends had been avoiding me. I remembered how we had whispered about the older girls who went off behind the baseball diamond. We knew how angry their mothers would have been if they had known.

"Come on," the boys said, "let's go."

"I told you she was a scairdy-cat."

I didn't answer them. No, I said to myself, she isn't a scairdy-cat. You may not like her and her girl friends may no longer like her but she likes herself too well to have an assigned boy friend.

"You don't have to be afraid of boys," my girl friend said, giggling. "Come with us, we've missed you."

"No," I said, "I don't want to. I'm not afraid of boys any longer. It's just that I want to meet a boy whom I will like and who will like me."

"That's just like you," they said. "You always think you're better than everyone else. The records we listen to aren't good enough for you; we don't study hard enough, and now our boys aren't nice enough for you."

"I didn't say that."

"No," they said, their voices rising, "but we could tell." They were shouting at me. They turned to the boys. "Bring her along. She'll run home and tell her mother. It's about time Miss Goody-Goody grew up."

The boys began pulling at my arms. They were hurting me. All I could hear was my friends screaming about how much they hated me. My knees became weak. I sank to the ground, more angry at my own weakness than at the people who were tormenting me. I felt the boys' grip loosen on my arms. From far off I heard one of the girls say, "She's fainted."

Maybe I have, I thought.

"She's only acting," a boy said. "Leave her here. She'll be all right. She's too scared to say anything."

I lay on the ground for what seemed a long time. I opened my eyes and saw I was alone. I stood up. I felt nothing—not anger . . . not hate . . . not fear. That's impossible, I thought. Maybe I'm dead. I started to laugh at my joke. I shook with laughter that I couldn't stop. I'm hysterical, I said over and over to myself, I must stop. Then I looked down and saw that my sweater and skirt were covered with dirt and leaves. The dirt was the final indignity. I felt anger begin to blot out my laughter and I wanted to hurt someone—anyone. Through my rage I seemed to be running about and flailing my arms, trying to get rid of the dirt that was on me. If only I could feel clean again I wouldn't have this wild anger.

Finally I was exhausted and began to sob. I cried very quietly to myself as I thought, this is what growing up means —to be alone and to be hurt. I can never return to being a little girl, but it's so hard to be alone and grown up.

I felt a touch on my arm and heard a boy's voice say, "Hello." My body stiffened. My skirt was dirty. Who was this boy? Of course, he felt free to try to pick me up in the park, the way I looked. I pulled my arm away without looking at him.

"Hello," he said again. "May I help you? You've been crying. Did you fall down?"

I walked a few steps away.

"No," he said, "you have a different kind of hurt. You didn't fall."

I turned to look at him full in the face. I had never known a boy who could say such a kind thing.

"Why are you looking at me?" he said, smiling.

I couldn't answer. I just shook my head.

"I'll tell you what," he said, "let's walk together a little way. Don't say a word. Any time you want to leave, just walk away and I promise I won't follow you. You're very pretty with the tears smudging your face. I'd like to walk with you."

I still couldn't say anything. I looked at his face again and there was such warmth and kindness there that without knowing it I gave him my hand like a little girl and we started walking together.

"I'm a senior," he said. "I see you all the time in school. I even remember when you started high school. I was a year ahead of you and I remember how tiny you looked carrying all those big books the first day. I wanted to ask you if I could help you but I was afraid my friends would make fun of me."

I spoke for the first time. "Do you worry about what your friends think? I don't any more."

"It depends," he said. "Yes, I worry about what my friends think. But I don't have friends any more who would laugh at me for helping a girl with a load of books."

"You're lucky," I said.

*There was a quiet assurance about this boy*

"No," he said, "I made it that way. I used to get very hurt because I had friends who would laugh at me every time I wanted to do something nice. They said I was a sissy. I even started believing it and trying to be like them but it didn't work. The harder I tried to be like them the more I wanted to be just like myself."

He started to walk down the path and I followed him. We walked slowly without saying a word. There was a quiet assurance about this boy that made walking with him very important for me. My hand felt so small in his. I liked the way his hand seemed to take mine inside it.

"I like holding hands with you," he said.

"This is the first time I've ever held hands with a boy," I told him. Then I felt very shy. "That was silly of me to say that."

"Why?" he asked.

"Because I must seem like a baby to you."

"I always thought that the girls who hold hands with everybody are the babies," he said. "They take something that is extra special and nice between two people and ruin it for themselves."

"My name is Melissa," I told him.

"Mine is Jacques," he replied.

We both laughed. Now we'd been introduced.

Then I noticed we were on the path to the baseball diamond. "I don't want to go there," I said.

"All right," he said. "I didn't know where this path led. Let's sit here on the grass awhile and then we'll go home. May I walk to school with you tomorrow?"

"Let's go behind the baseball diamond," I said.

"Why did you change your mind?"

"Because my friends are there and I'm going to show them that I'm not afraid."

"That's not flattering to me," he said, "but if you really want to go I'll take you there. But think about it. Should you do anything just to show anyone or prove something?"

I began to cry. "Thank you," I said. "I guess I really am acting foolishly. Do you know why I'm crying? It's because you're so nice. Now isn't that a foolish reason to cry?"

He didn't say anything, but he looked at me with such understanding that I had to go on. I told him all about what had happened that afternoon. He was very angry. "That's terrible. Why do people have to hurt one another? Why isn't there an easier way to grow up?"

"Do you really think I'm grown up?" I was afraid to look at him while I waited for his answer.

"Do you?" he asked.

"Yes," I said. "I like it."

*I began to cry*

He smiled and lay down on the grass and looked up at the sky. I sat next to him.

"You see that bird?" The boy pointed by moving his chin. "He was very happy when he was young. He used to spend all his time in the nest and every day his mother would fly away and come back with food. Then one day his mother pushed him out of his nest. He was very frightened as he fell from the tree but some instinct made him begin beating his wings and soon he saw that he could fly like his mother. He was thrilled. He flew as high as he could and began singing and singing because now he could fly and find food and make a nest for his children. It happens to all birds. I wonder why it doesn't happen to all humans? Most humans never learn to fly. They spend all their time trying to climb back to the nest they fell from. You're one of the lucky ones, Melissa. You fell and you flew. Now all you need is more practice. Wow!" he said. "That was philosophical."

"It was beautiful," I said.

"What time do you leave for school?" he asked. "I'll meet you."

"Eight-thirty," I muttered drowsily. It's so nice being with a boy, I thought; so nice and so natural.

# A Midsummer Night's Dream

Thinking about growing up in the ballet *Still Point* turned my thoughts to myself as a woman outside the theater. The years had gone by since I left Toronto, and from a young ballet student I had become a ballerina of the New York City Ballet. From a girl who had lived alone in a small women's residence hall I had become a wife and mother. I had never thought about my life or planned it, but somehow I had achieved a happy blend of home and career. I was very fortunate. It is time I started to think about my life, I told myself. I wanted to plan my future so that my life would continue to be as happy as it was then.

The only thing all of us in my family wanted was a little girl. Just as I had always wanted a brother when I was a child, Stuart wanted a sister. And Don, like every father, wanted a little girl he could pamper and spoil. I began to think about taking another vacation from dancing and presenting the two men in my family with a sister and a daughter.

My career was a more difficult problem. I enjoyed most dancing with the New York City Ballet in ballets choreographed by Mr. Balanchine. I had the most audience success with other companies in works by other choreographers. I kept thinking that I would soon have to choose between the two and I didn't know which was more important to me—my own artistic satisfaction or the applause and bravos of the audience.

This situation was puzzling to me. Before I made any choice, I wanted to look at the ballets objectively, as a member of the audience would, so that I could understand the differences and make a more intelligent decision.

Balanchine is primarily a musical choreographer. Using each dancer as an instrument in the orchestra, he translates the sound of the music into visual movement on the stage. To enjoy Balanchine choreography, the audience must look at the stage as a whole and not focus on any one dancer or group of dancers. To watch just the principal dancers would be as unsatisfying as to listen to only one instrument in a symphony orchestra. The girl in the last row of the corps de ballet, posed motionless, is as much a part of the musical choreography as the ballerina doing a mélange of intricate steps.

This makes for a dilemma on the part of the principal dancers. To dance Balanchine's ballets successfully, we must often subordinate our personalities and blend with all the other dancers on stage. To do this means that the audience will not see us as individuals.

In ballets of other choreographers and especially story ballets the opposite is true. The principal dancer is usually the central character. She carries the dramatic line. The audience is continuously watching her to find out what will happen next in the story. Most often the choreographer has to sacrifice movement to the integrity of the story so that the movements are not as difficult or beautiful or satisfying to dance. Despite this, the principal dancer receives more recognition simply because it is she and she alone the audience has been watching.

That is all very well, I thought. Now I understand why I seem to have so much more success outside of Balanchine ballets but that doesn't help me decide the future direction I want to take with my career.

The more I thought about what I wanted to do, the more confused I became. I spent almost a year trying to decide what was right for me. I would accept a guest-star engagement with another company and then miss terribly the challenge of working with Balanchine. I would return to the New York City Ballet and miss the excitement of an audience cheering. I solved nothing except to realize that there was no place where I could have everything I wanted. I knew I would have to make a decision and I wanted to put off the choice.

I was in California on tour with another ballet company when the need for immediate action was taken out of my hands. I had been feeling very tired on tour but, instead of being impatient with myself as I am when my body does not feel completely alive, I had a warm feeling of contentment. I was perfectly happy to sleep late and miss my daily class. The only time I felt like that was seven years before when I was to be a mother for the first time. I wondered.

Soon I knew for sure. I was going to be a mother again. I went to the head of the company and told her the good news and that I would be leaving soon for home. As a woman she was overjoyed. As the head of a company with two months of future bookings, at all of which I was expected to perform, she knew she would have many problems to deal with. Her warmth as a woman won out and we spent a delightful few hours in my hotel room, I packing and she lying on the bed while we talked about our families.

When I got home Stuart and Don were excited. We were all convinced the new arrival was to be a girl. We thought only of girls' names and when we changed the spare room to a nursery we painted it pink. We spent the next months together without the distraction of my rushing to class in the morning or performing in the evening. And I never once thought about dancing. My career for those months was my home and family and I loved every moment of it.

Stuart, with the frankness only a young child can have, provided the only disquieting note. "Mommy," he said, "what if Jennifer is a boy? Then what will we call her?" Jennifer was the name we had decided upon for our little girl. Both Don and I had thought about this and always dismissed it from our minds. Somehow we thought by not mentioning our doubts they would not take shape in reality.

Jennifer was born. Don walked around for a full week smiling quietly to himself and Stuart announced to one and all at school, in the playground, and on the street that he had a little sister with beautiful brown curly hair and the largest brown eyes anyone had ever seen.

I never felt more content. A perfect family. An older brother and a younger sister and everybody happy with one another. For a time I considered retiring from dancing so that I would never have to leave the joy I felt in being a part of my family. But I knew I would dance again. Dancing was not as important to me as my family but it was a part of me just as they were.

The first day I began to practice after my long rest I was frightened. My muscles would not obey my commands. It had been such a long time since I had last taken a vacation from dancing that I forgot what happens to my body after a prolonged period without work. My muscles are so finely trained and such exacting demands are made on them that I must work every day to keep them at performance edge. Even a few days without work means that I need a corresponding few days to get back to peak performance. When I remembered that I had not danced or taken a class for more than six months I felt better about my weakened state but I was determined to regain my mastery over my body.

I worked alone for more than a month to gain more control before I went to an actual class. When I did go to the School of American Ballet I did not take the professional class. I studied with the intermediates because the steps they were taught were slower and less complicated.

When I was nearly ready to perform I told Mr. Balanchine I would soon be able to rejoin the company. He was very pleased because he was planning a new full-length ballet based on Shakespeare's *Midsummer Night's Dream* and he wanted me to appear in it. He was very considerate. He knew it would be impossible for me to have my full strength and told me I should program myself whenever I wanted to dance. "You will need the performances as well as the classes to regain your strength," he said, "but you know yourself best so you must dance only what will help you and what you are ready to perform." Then we discussed the new ballet. There were two parts in the ballet which I could dance. There was Titania, the Queen of the Fairies. It was an acting-dancing role such has Balanchine rarely choreographs. Titania carries the story line and when she is on stage all eyes are focused on her.

But there was also a lovely pas de deux in the second act which was not part of the story and was the kind of dancing I

*I worked alone for more than a month to gain more control before I went to an actual class*

loved most. Mr. B had choreographed a sustained series of balances and lines for the ballerina and her partner which underscored the delicate strains of the Mendelssohn music. The dancers on stage became a central theme which the music played about, now over, now under, with the dancers adding strength to the airiness of the musical game. It was a difficult pas de deux because it had to be danced perfectly. An awkward line or technical error would destroy the light balance between dancer and music. There were no tricks or feats of bravura. A completely successful performance would leave the audience with the feeling that they had just viewed the loveliest but simplest-to-dance pas de deux of all time.

I asked Mr. Balanchine if I could dance the pas de deux. As my strength returned I felt such a divine pleasure in feeling my body dance again that I was convinced that all I wanted was to dance for the pure pleasure of my own enjoyment. I thought I had finally reached a decision about my career.

But I was soon to understand that circumstances would not allow me to be at peace with my decision. The girl who was chosen to dance Titania was injured during rehearsal and I was scheduled to dance Titania opening night.

I alternated during the rehearsal weeks between learning Titania's part and learning the pas de deux. The parts were completely different and each represented the different areas of dance I thought I had made a choice between. And, maddeningly, I loved each part in a different way and always missed the one while I was dancing the other. Finally I realized that the reason I was unhappy then and had been unhappy before was that when I was dancing one type of ballet I always thought about the other. From now on, I thought, I will enjoy whatever I am doing. I love to dance and if I do not create decisions for myself to make I can have pleasure from every type of ballet. I could enjoy Titania for the acting and dancing ability

I could bring to the role. I could enjoy the pas de deux for the artistic satisfaction I experienced. I looked forward to opening night because I knew how Titania must feel as she ruled her land of the fairies. I had my own kingdom to rule. I felt like a queen in my new-found understanding of myself.

## The Story

Everyone thinks being a fairy queen is an easy task, just waving magic wands and dancing on moonbeams and the like. Well, it is not that way at all and if anyone should know it is I, Titania, the Queen of the fairies. There is a great deal of responsibility in my profession. I must supervise my whole host of tiny subjects as they travel about the world each day to see that the dew is on the grass and that the flowers blossom into loveliness.

My husband Oberon, the King of the fairies, helps me a great deal with my duties. We love each other very much but sometimes, like all husbands and wives, we quarrel with each other.

Many of our disagreements are about a friend of my husband's whose name is Puck. Puck is a mischief-maker. Instead of helping people as all good fairies should, he thinks it is

Puck and a group of fairies

*Oberon and his court*

funny to cause confusion among the mortals. I am always telling Oberon that he should be stricter with him but I must admit that I find Puck amusing as well. He is always sorry for the mischief he causes and when things go too far, as they sometimes do, he bustles about setting everything right again.

One time he and Oberon played a trick on me. I laughed with them when they told me about it later but if I had known about it at the time I would not have thought it was so funny.

My husband and I were having a silly quarrel and both of us were too stubborn to give in. I had adopted a little boy and made him a part of my fairy band. The child was very striking, with jet-black skin which complemented my own fair features. I taught him to carry the train of my dress and wherever we went we caused a stir in the fairy world.

Oberon became jealous of this attention and wanted the boy for his own. He kept asking me for him and I kept refusing. Finally we exchanged some bitter words and each of us went angrily away.

I would have forgiven him but we were to have left our home the next day to be present at a wedding in ancient Athens. Part of our duties is to attend important weddings and bless the bride and groom. We like to go to these weddings to-

*We exchanged some bitter words*

Hippolyta, the Queen of the Amazons

*Dancing with one of my subjects*

gether because they are such happy times and remind us of our own love. When I learned that Oberon, out of spite, intended to travel to the wedding without me I was very hurt and angry.

I arrived in Athens and tried to avoid Oberon but we met by chance in the large woods outside of town. There the quarrel started again.

Oberon imperiously demanded that I give him the child. He must have been at a loss for words, for he began his "I am your lord and master" speech and he knows that is the surest way to infuriate me even when I am in a good mood. I did not answer

*Dancing with one of my subjects*

him, which I know makes him angriest. He stormed off vowing he would take the child from me.

When he was out of earshot he and Puck devised a plan to part me from the child. Puck was sent in search of the magic flower of love, a drop of whose nectar, placed on the eyelids of a sleeping person, causes him to love the first thing he sees upon awakening. The plan was to cause me to love a creature so grotesque that I could be shamed into parting with the child because of my infatuation.

While Puck was searching the world for the flower Oberon

*They had fallen in love in such a way as to make each of them unhappy*

saw two young couples enter the woods. They were most
unhappy. Each loved the one who loved the other. Oberon,
who is very romantic, was so concerned about them that, when
Puck returned, he postponed his own plans until he could help
the young lovers. He told Puck to wait for them to become tired
of their wandering and fall asleep, and then use some of the
nectar from the flower to set their loves aright. Believing that
Puck could carry out so simple a task, Oberon once again
concentrated on his scheme to bewitch me.

It was late at night. All my fairies were about me dancing
and playing at the end of their day's chores. I had curled up
in my sea-shell throne to sleep so that I would be bright and

fresh to spread the morning sunshine over the countryside.

While I was sleeping Oberon quietly sprinkled a drop from the flower on my eyelids. Meanwhile Puck searched for a strange and ridiculous creature for me to love.

Fate played into Puck's hands. A group of tradesmen had come into the woods. Puck, on spying them, decided to combine mischief with pleasure and, having led one away from the others, changed the man's head to that of a donkey.

The poor man was very frightened. He knew something had happened to him, but he did not know what. He began to sing a little song to keep up his courage. The song woke me and at first I thought it was the most awful noise I had ever heard. But then I spied him and the magic spell was so strong that even his braying noises sounded like melodious music. And as for his donkey's head, I thought he was the handsomest creature in the entire world.

I summoned all my fairies to me and told them that henceforth the donkey would be my constant companion. Together we covered him with garlands of flowers and catered to his every wish. Whenever I looked at him I could not help caressing his face or kissing him gently on the check. It must have been a trying time for my subjects to see me paying so much attention to a funny-looking donkey.

Puck returned to Oberon to tell him of the success of their trick and found him very upset. The lovers had awakened and were more unhappy than they had been before. Puck had been confused and instead of arranging them in the proper pairs had caused both men to love the same woman. My husband and his friend stood transfixed, not knowing what to do as the men were challenging each other to a duel and the women were sobbing helplessly nearby.

Oberon was the first to gain his composure. He wanted to

*I could not stop from kissing him gently*

*It must have been a trying time for my subjects to see me paying so much attention to a funny-looking donkey*

get to my side before the charade with the donkey could go any further and at the same time he knew he could not leave the four young people in their dilemma. Quickly he instructed Puck as to what he wanted done and told him that this time he had better do it right. Then he rushed to the clearing where my court and I were still entertaining our guest.

Puck, under cover of night, imitated first the voice of one man and then the voice of the other, shouting insults and hurling challenges at both. He led them in opposite directions, each one trying to catch the other until they became so exhausted that they sank to the ground and slept. Then he anointed their eyelids again with the nectar from the flower

*The lovers were awakened and were more unhappy than they had been before*

*Puck was challenging each of them to a duel*

and, making sure that this time there would be no mistake, arranged the lovers happily together.

Oberon came upon me in the clearing and pretended to be shocked at what he saw. With all seriousness he upbraided me for being so foolish as to become enamored of a donkey. I still had no idea that this was any of his doing and kept begging his forgiveness and asking his patience with me, for despite everything he said the magic was so strong that I still thought the donkey was the most beautiful creature I had ever seen.

How Oberon must have laughed as he granted me his for-

*The lovers happily together*

giveness and patience if I would merely show him my good
faith by giving him the child! I was so ashamed, I would have
done anything if only he would not be angry and I consented
to give him the child. Before I could change my mind he had
the boy transported to his kingdom. Then he changed the
donkey back to a human being and removed the spell from me.

The sun was rising over the woods as I stood confused before
Oberon. I tried to regain my queenly composure but I was so
troubled by what I thought was a dream that I could only
stand there and ask my husband meekly what had happened.

He wouldn't tell me. He only said he was glad we were no

longer quarreling and that from now on whenever we had a disagreement we would talk about it reasonably and never be angry at each other again. I loved him very much then. I was glad I had given him the child.

Hand in hand my husband and I stood while we watched the sunlight wake the lovers from their sleep. They were too busy with their loves to remember the anger of the night before, which seemed like a faint dream played against the happiness of the morning. Their love did more to brighten the clearing than all my fairies had they worked the sun around.

Even Puck was touched. As the happy couples left Puck was busy sweeping the remains of all our dreams from the clearing, hiding them under the flowers and the blades of grass. For everyone's dream is his very own and it would never do for it to be found by another.